D0282810

A Century of
Labour

A History of the Labour Party 1900–2000

Keith Laybourn

SUTTON PUBLISHING

First published in 2000 by
Sutton Publishing Limited · Phoenix Mill
Thrupp · Stroud · Gloucestershire · GL5 2BU

Copyright © Keith Laybourn, 2000

All rights reserved. No part of this publication may be reproduced, stored in a retrieval system, or transmitted, in any form, or by any means, electronic, mechanical, photocopying, recording or otherwise, without the prior permission of the publisher and copyright holder.

Keith Laybourn has asserted the moral right to be identified as the author of this work.

British Library Cataloguing in Publication Data
A catalogue record for this book is available from the British Library

ISBN 0-7509-2305-9

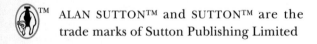
ᵀᴹ ALAN SUTTON™ and SUTTON™ are the
trade marks of Sutton Publishing Limited

Typeset in 10/13 pt New Baskerville.
Typesetting and origination by
Sutton Publishing Limited.
Printed in Great Britain by
Biddles Limited, Guildford, Surrey.

Contents

List of Illustrations

Acknowledgements

There have been many people who, over many years, have contributed to the research that I have conducted into the British Labour movement and the British Labour Party. Pride of place among them must go to Jack Reynolds (1915–88), who first taught me about the Independent Labour Party and the Labour Party while I was a student at the University of Bradford between 1964 and 1967. In addition, Stephen Bird, Andrew Flinn and Philip Dunn, of the National Museum of Labour History, have been immensely helpful in guiding me to the Labour records and photographs that have formed the basis of this book. The late David Wright, the late David James, Tony Jowitt, Peter Wood, David Taylor and Peter Gurney have also given me guidance and encouragement. I would also like to thank Christopher Feeney and Sarah Moore, both of Sutton Publishing, for their great help and guidance in the production of this book. The photographs in this collection come from the Labour Party Archive at the National Museum of Labour History.

Abbreviations

ASE	Amalgamated Society of Engineers
ASRS	Amalgamated Society of Railway Servants
BMA	British Medical Association
BUF	British Union of Fascists
CLPD	Campaign for Labour Party Democracy
CPGB	Communist Party of Great Britain
EEC	European Economic Community
ILP	Independent Labour Party
IRA	Irish Republican Army
LEA	Labour Electoral Association
LCC	Labour Coordinating Committee
LRC	Labour Representation Committee
MFGB	Miners' Federation of Great Britain
NAC	National Administrative Council (of the ILP)
NATO	North Atlantic Treaty Organization
NCB	National Coal Board
NEC	National Executive Committee (of the Labour Party)
NFRB	National Fabian Research Bureau
NHS	National Health Service
NUM	National Union of Mineworkers
NUR	National Union of Railwaymen
OMOV	One Member One Vote
PLP	Parliamentary Labour Party
SDF	Social Democratic Federation
SDP	Social Democratic Party
SLL	Socialist Labour League
TUC	Trades Union Congress
UDC	Union of Democratic Control
WEC	War Emergency Committee
WSPU	Women's Social and Political Union

Introduction

The Labour Party was formed, as the Labour Representation Committee (LRC), at Memorial Hall, Farringdon Street, London on 27 February 1900. At first there was no obvious sign that it would be any more successful than previous efforts to form parties of the working classes or socialist organizations. Indeed, at first the omens did not look good. Its initial home was the back room of Ramsay MacDonald's London flat at 3 Lincoln's Inn Fields, and it spent only £33 in supporting fifteen candidates at the 1900 general election. Only two of them, James Keir Hardie for Merthyr and Richard Bell for Derby, were returned as MPs. Yet it had one advantage, which the quasi-Marxist Social Democratic Federation (SDF), the middle-class socialist Fabian Society, and even the partly trade-union and working-class based Independent Labour Party (ILP) did not have – access to mass trade-union support.

Neither the SDF nor the Fabians had sought the support of the trade unions, and in the 1890s the ILP operated in a climate where trade unions were hesitant and often hostile about giving their political support to socialist organizations. Indeed, many of the craft trade unions and the associations of semi-skilled workers were dominated by Liberal and Conservative leaders. James Maudsley, for instance, was the Conservative leader of the Amalgamated Society of Cotton Spinners and Benjamin Pickard was the Liberal leader of both the Yorkshire Miners' Association and the Miners' Federation of Great Britain (MFGB). Thus the moment did not seem propitious for the foundation of a non-socialist independent party that wished to represent the interests of the working classes. Yet within six years the LRC, the early Labour Party, was able to secure twenty-nine, soon to be thirty, seats in the House of Commons. What had changed? Why did the working-class voter abandon the Liberal and Conservative parties, the 'Yellow and Blue Tories' as they were dubbed by the Bradford ILP leaders during the 1895 general election?

From the 1860s onwards representation of the working-class voter had been increasing. The second parliamentary Reform Act was passed in 1867 and the third in 1884. This meant that more than 50 per cent of working men, though not women, had the franchise by 1900. In addition, there had been local government reforms, in the 1860s and the 1880s, that reduced the qualification to ratepayers of one year's standing, widened the franchise, and removed the property qualifications previously necessary for candidates to stand in local elections. If there is one good reason why the Labour Party could not have emerged much before the 1890s it is to be found in the fact that property qualification, by and large, would have restricted their representation to middle-class candidates. By 1900, then, there was a substantial working-class vote to be organized and the prospect of working-class candidates.

At first the new working-class vote was absorbed by the Liberal and Conservative parties. Both parties set up working men's clubs and claimed, in their various ways, the vote of the working man. Not surprisingly, Alfred Illingworth, the dominating Bradford Liberal leader and sometime MP for Bradford, reflected often that he was the true representative of working-class opinion and that the working men should blindly follow his lead. This was an attitude widely adopted by the Liberal leaders throughout the country. To them the Newcastle Programme (1891) of social reform designed to bring the working classes more firmly within the Liberal Party meant little. One Independent Labour Party writer remarked of the Bradford Liberal Association that

> It selects candidates, and decides how far these candidates shall go in their advocacy of reform. To this section the Newcastle Programme counts for nothing unless it is considered of use in gaining votes at election times. Its proposed reforms are never advocated by official Liberals, and anyone who takes a very prominent part in keeping its items before the public is cold-shouldered.[1]

The Liberal argument was that Home Rule for Ireland must be achieved before social reform could be offered, but that only made the Liberal neglect of working-class interests more marked because on that basis social reform was likely to be a long way off. The result was that Liberalism had a declining appeal to the politically conscious working man. Katherine St John Conway maintained that 'In London, he [the working man] listens to the persuasive reasoning of the Progressives – in the provinces, face to face with the Liberals of the Illingworth [Bradford], Kitson [Leeds] and Pease [Newcastle] type, he is doggedly independent.'[2] The situation with the Conservative Party, which simply offered its traditional appeal to monarchy and empire, was little better; it was not even attempting to make an appeal to its working-class voters.

There was increasing frustration among some sections of the working classes at the failure of the Liberals and Conservatives to respond to the rising demands of the working-class electorate. Yet there was little evidence, except in a few small areas, that the old two-party system was about to be changed. The formation of the Labour Representation Committee seemed to make little difference. Yet its fortunes were transformed by the Taff Vale Case (1900–1) which, in removing the legal protection of trade-union funds in strikes, encouraged many trade unionists to seek the political support of the LRC rather than the Liberal or Conservative parties.

Since then, trade-union support has always been of significant importance to the growth of Labour, although the relations between the LRC/Labour Party and the trade unions has often been contentious, not least because Labour in government has often gone its own separate way from the trade unions. Nevertheless, until the end of the twentieth century, at least until Tony Blair's recent moves to distance the 1997 Labour government from the trade unions, the Labour Party and the Trades Union Congress (TUC) have often worked in close harness while recognizing that they normally operate in different spheres of interest.

If that has been the basic relationship within the Labour movement one must also note that there have been countervailing tendencies. The most obvious is that the Labour Party has, increasingly, become more professional and middle class in its political composition. This was partly evident in the return of James Ramsay MacDonald and Philip Snowden in the 1906 general election. Neither of them were trade unionists, and both were effectively professional politicians who wished the embryonic Labour Party to be more than simply a party of the trade unions and the working classes. To both these leading political figures, the Labour Party was to be a party of all classes. Although trade unions have sponsored Labour MPs from the beginning, this relationship has fluctuated over time and has often become more notional than real. It is in the tensions between the trade unions and the more professional political sections of the Labour Party that one can see the problems that led to events such as the end of the second Labour government and the formation of the National government in August 1931; in other words, the events surrounding the 'betrayal' of the Labour Party by Ramsay MacDonald.

There have also been serious tensions within the Labour Party on other issues. Most obviously, the conflict between collectivism and individualism. This can be seen in the tensions between the individualist socialism of Philip Snowden and the collectivist spirit of the trade unions. Snowden envisaged the role of socialist society as releasing people to enjoy a healthier and more varied personal lifestyle, which he described in the lecture and pamphlet *The Individual Under Socialism.* The trade unions, however, emphasized the need for joint action and the need for state control of the means of production in order to ensure the more equitable distribution of wealth and income which socialism demanded. The conflict was one of the means by which socialism could be brought about in a reformist manner. In the end, however, it was the trade union, and Fabian, collectivist, viewpoint that was put forward with the introduction of Clause Four to the constitution of the Labour Party in 1918, the original (it was amended in 1928) form of which ran:

> To secure for producers by hand or by brain the full fruits of their industry, and the most equitable distribution thereof that may be possible, upon the basis of the Common Ownership of the Means of Production and the best obtainable system of popular administration and control of each industry and service.

These tensions were also evident in the conflict between the trade-union support for Clause Four in the 1950s and the efforts of Tony Crosland and Hugh Gaitskell to remove it in favour of the creation of a fairer society, based upon redistribution of wealth and income through higher taxation and more state social provision. More recently there has been discord between Tony Blair's new 'Third Way' approach to Labour (drawing upon both public and private involvement in the economy) and the Old Labour and trade-union concern about New Labour's abandonment of Clause Four and, more obviously, the idea that the state can intervene to generate full employment. These tensions and issues on the meaning of function of Labour's socialism are examined in this book.

Chapter One deals with the formation of the Labour Representation Committee in 1900 and the Labour Party in 1906 and asks the vital question – why did the Labour Party emerge so fully before 1914? Was it because of the failure of the Liberal Party to properly represent the interests of Labour or because the Liberal Party maintained Labour as its progressive arm. This flows into Chapter Two where the issue is whether or not Labour overtook the Liberals as a result of the First World War or despite it. Some historians have stressed the importance of the war in dividing the Liberal Party, seen in the replacement of Herbert Asquith by David Lloyd George in December 1916, while others suggest that Labour was growing rapidly regardless of the war, reorganizing its structure, redefining its policies in socialist terms, and realigning its position with the other political parties.

The Labour Party formed its first, minority, government in 1924 and its second, minority, government in 1929. But why had it emerged so rapidly to become a party of government? Was it because, despite Labour's poor organization, the other political parties failed to staunch its progress, because of the development of 'class politics', with the working class associating themselves with the Labour Party, or because of the political skills of James Ramsay MacDonald, Labour's leader? Of course, this growth all came to an abrupt end when MacDonald abandoned the second Labour government in August 1931 and helped form a National government. Why did he do this? Was it because he wished to renounce his former associates or was he driven by circumstances? Labour's growth in the 1920s and the debacle of 1931 are therefore the focus of Chapter Three. Chapter Four examines the way in which the Labour Party revived quickly so that within fourteen years of the collapse of the second Labour government, and the enormous political losses of the 1931 general election, it was able to return to power under Attlee and with a landslide victory in 1945? Why was this? Was it because Labour was not fundamentally damaged by the events of 1931, because it had redesigned and developed its socialist policies, or because of its experience in government during the Second World War? It may even be that the British electorate saw more prospect of social and welfare reforms being introduced by Labour than by Winston Churchill's Conservative Party.

Chapter Five deals with what many observers would regard as the highpoint of Labour's achievements, its creation of the modern welfare state during the early years of the Attlee administrations of 1945 to 1951. The main concern here, has been to explain why the welfare state emerged as it did, whether it was a product of the Beveridge Report of 1942, or the result of Labour policies developed and defined in the 1930s? There is, of course, the possibility that it was the product of both.

The years from 1951 to 1994, if not 1997, have, in many ways, been seen as years of crisis for Labour. From 1951 to 1964, Labour was the opposition in the House of Commons and there was some concern that they might never form a government again. This certainly led to internal conflict within the Party between Tony Crosland and Hugh Gaitskell, on the one hand, and the trade unions on the other. Should the Party continue with its commitment to public ownership through Clause Four or should it abandon it and develop a fairer and more liberal society through the operation of both private and public activity? Gaitskell's attempt to reform the Party failed and he died before Labour came to power again. However, Labour formed governments again between 1964 and 1970 and between 1974 and 1979, under the leadership of Harold Wilson and James Callaghan. Yet these governments were not the most successful in terms of economic growth, financial stability and strikes, and Labour was back in opposition between 1979 and 1997.

Labour held office for only eleven of the forty-six years between 1951 and 1997. It is not surprising, then, that various writers and politicians should have asked the generic question, posed in the title of one pamphlet produced in 1960, 'Must Labour Lose?'. Chapter Six deals with the period 1951 to 1979 when it appeared that Labour was failing to develop its policies to meet the needs of a changing society. Chapter Seven deals with the years between 1979 and 1994 when, after the despair of the leadership failures of Michael Foot, and the problems of dealing with Militant Tendency, the Party began to recover under the leadership of Neil Kinnock and John Smith. They reorganized the Party and reduced the influence of trade unions, although there was still much doubt whether Labour would ever again form another government, especially when it appeared the more popular party in the 1987 and 1992 campaigns but still could not win the elections. The turning point came with the election of Tony Blair as Labour leader in 1994. Riding upon a wave of popular support this charismatic leader forced the Labour Party to abandon Clause Four, to combat the suggestion that Labour was merely the agency of the trade unions, and develop the New Labour bandwagon of the 'Third Way', building an economy based upon both public and private initiatives. This development, anathema to many Old Labour supporters raised upon the close connections between the trade unions and the Labour Party, forms the basis of Chapter Eight. There is also some assessment of the role of New Labour in office since May 1997.

The main argument presented in this book is that the Labour Party developed in the first part of the century because of its close alliance with the trade unions. This was both an advantage and a disadvantage – providing resources for Labour but controlling and limiting its policies. In the second half of the century there has been a move away from trade-union influence as the Labour Party has come to believe that socialism has to be more than Clause Four and as it is increasingly recognized that Labour must be, what Ramsay MacDonald always saw it as being, a party of the whole nation and every class rather than a party of just the working class and trade unions. These changes have been at a cost of 'class loyalty' and socialism. As the Labour Party reaches its centenary it is not at all clear what New Labour has put in its place. All that is certain is that the Labour Party looks highly electable now but has lost its distinctive socialist qualities and become more of a progressive political party of the centre offering policies which lack the ideological commitment and clear definition of Old Labour or Old Socialism. This may reflect the general decline of European socialism, or Eurosocialism, that has occurred at the end of the twentieth century. Certainly, there has been a move to the centre in politics, but the policies Blair is advocating lack any major commitment to the redistribution of wealth and income and emphasize the need to work with a capitalist system which does not reward people equally. It is hardly surprising that there is tension between Blair's 'New Labour' and 'Old Labour'.

CHAPTER ONE

The Rise of Labour

Foundation of the Labour Representation Committee and Development of the Party, *c.* 1900–18

THE PIONEERS

The British Labour Party emerged from a variety of socialist and working-class traditions that had developed in the 1880s and 1890s. There were three major strands. Firstly, there were the quasi-Marxist organizations, most obviously the Social Democratic Federation, formed as the Democratic Federation in 1881 before assuming its new title in 1884, led by Henry Mayers Hyndman, and the Socialist League, formed in December 1884, and led by William Morris, the socialist artist, poet and designer. Both movements were committed to revolutionary change but attracted limited political support at first, although the SDF did increase its membership substantially in the decade before the First World War. Briefly, from 1900 to 1901, it was affiliated to the Labour Representation Committee (the early Labour Party).

Secondly, there were several socialist organizations committed to gradual reform through parliamentary or local action. The most obvious of these were the Fabian Society and the Independent Labour Party. The Fabians were formed in January 1884 and, at the national level, brought together a number of distinguished poets, writers and civil servants, such as Sidney Webb, Sidney Olivier and George Bernard Shaw who, after showing an initial interest in Marxism, became dedicated gradualists. The Fabian approach was to play down the importance of the class conflict which Marxists envisaged and to stress the need to extend gradually the control of the state and municipal authorities to redress the economic inequality in British society. The Independent Labour Party, which was formed at Bradford in January 1893, broadly accepted the Fabian approach but was more overtly working class and trade union in its support and orientation and generally espoused an ethical and moral attitude to socialism, based upon the assumption that the inequalities of income and wealth in Britain were morally wrong. In its early years, it was dominated by James Keir Hardie, the Scottish miners' leader who, in 1892, became the first socialist returned to Parliament when he won the West Ham South seat. Other political figures, most obviously Philip Snowden from Keighley, and James Ramsay MacDonald, from Scotland, gradually emerged through the ranks of the Independent Labour Party before becoming prominent figures in the parliamentary Labour Party – Snowden becoming Labour's first Chancellor of the Exchequer and MacDonald becoming Labour's first Prime Minister. Both the Fabians and the Independent Labour Party joined the Labour Representation Committee in 1900.

Thirdly, there was the trade-union movement, which became associated with the Independent Labour Party from the early 1890s. Although many of the larger trade-union organizations, such as the Miners' Federation of Great Britain, remained connected with the Liberal Party until the eve of the First World War, some of the newer ones, such as the Gasworkers and General Labourers, were dominated by socialist activists and linked with the Independent Labour Party from the early 1890s. Industrial disputes such as the Great London Dock Strike of 1889 and the Manningham Mills strike, of Bradford woollen and worsted textile workers, in 1890–1, ensured that many of the members of the new trade unions saw themselves as the 'reverse side of the Independent Labour Party coin'.[1] In the years between 1900 and 1914, the trade-union membership of the Independent Labour Party increased, as did that of the, still non-socialist but independent labour, Labour Representation Committee – even though a substantial proportion of the trade-union movement and those unions affiliated to the Trades Union Congress (formed in 1868) still favoured the Liberal and Conservative parties.

These three strands of support for independent working-class politics conflated in 1900 to form the Labour Representation Committee, the early Labour Party. February 1900 was, therefore, a unique moment in British Labour history.

THE FORMATION OF THE LABOUR REPRESENTATION COMMITTEE, 27–8 FEBRUARY 1900

The idea of forming a Labour Representation Committee (LRC) had first emerged in the late 1890s, arising from the joint effort of socialist societies and the Trades Union Congress (TUC). The TUC passed a resolution in 1898 calling for the working classes to support socialist parties. At the same time the Independent Labour Party (ILP) approached the TUC and the Scottish TUC to take 'united political action'. Eventually, in 1899, the executive of the Amalgamated Society of Railway Servants (ASRS) urged that the Parliamentary Committee of the TUC should examine the ways in which it could increase the number of Labour MPs in the next Parliament. The 1899 TUC Conference accepted the idea by a narrow majority and a voluntary meeting was arranged between the delegates of 570,000 trade unionists (less than half the membership of the TUC) and the representatives of the ILP, the SDF and the Fabians.

Ultimately, the Labour Party emerged as the LRC at a conference held in Memorial Hall, Farringdon Street, London, on 27 and 28 February 1900, with James Ramsay MacDonald, a prominent member of the Independent Labour Party and future Labour Prime Minister, as its secretary. Addressing the 129 delegates the Chairman, W.C. Steadman, a Radical Liberal MP and trade unionist, announced that:

> For the first time in the history of the Labour movement all sections in that movement will be drawn together in this Conference. Whether they formed a Labour Party or allied themselves to other political parties in the House of Commons, let them be represented by men of character.[2]

This statement indicated two essential features in the early development of an independent Labour Party. The first is that the LRC brought together the various strands of the wider Labour movement for the first time. This itself presented real problems since the trade unions were still very much influenced by the Liberals while socialist parties, such as the Independent Labour Party (ILP), wanted political independence. The second is that not all those present were certain whether or not the envisaged organization would be merely an interest group or a genuinely independent political party. James Keir Hardie, who had represented

West Ham South in Parliament between 1892 and 1895, had no such doubts for he committed the conference to political independence with the successful amendment:

> That this Conference is in favour of establishing a distinct Labour group in the House of Commons, who shall have their own whips, and agree upon a policy which must embrace a resolution to co-operate with any party which for the time being may be engaged in promoting legislation in the direct interests of labour, and be equally ready to associate themselves with any party in opposing measures having the opposite tendency. . . .[3]

Thus, to Hardie, the LRC was going to be an independent Labour Party willing to compromise with other parties on the promotion of working-class interests. Hardie's resolution set the tone of the LRC/Labour Party for the next eighteen years, until its 1918 constitution committed it to socialism. Indeed, Hardie's approach was one he had been adopting ever since his own unsuccessful attempt to win the Mid-Lanark parliamentary by-election in April 1888. On the one hand he advocated political independence, but on the other lay the contradictory ambition of participating in a broader political realignment in British politics.

At this stage, Hardie's political ambitions seemed rather optimistic given that there were no LRC or independent Labour MPs in Parliament at that time. Nevertheless, during the next quarter of a century the LRC/Labour Party developed to a position where it was able to form a minority Labour government in 1924. Much of this growth represents the unleashing of political opportunities for the working class and the trade union movement, and to changes in the ideology of the Party. It has also been a product of leadership, the 'men of character' alluded to by Steadman.

THE GROWTH OF THE LABOUR REPRESENTATION COMMITTEE 1900–6

At first the prospects for the LRC did not look good. In the 1900 general election, Hardie was returned for Merthyr and Richard Bell for Derby but this was a poor return for all the effort involved, although the fifteen Labour candidates averaged about 4,000 votes each. What helped to change the LRC's fortunes, however, was the decision of the House of

Lords, in July 1901, to uphold the claim made by the Taff Vale Railway Company against the ASRS for £23,000 of financial damages incurred by its members during a strike. The decision exposed all unions' funds to similar claims. In this, and other cases, the House of Lords had stripped away the financial impunity of the trade unions. With one fell swoop, the Lords had given added impetus to the demand for independent parliamentary representation for the working classes and strengthened the case of the LRC. A Liberal intellectual stated 'that which no Socialist writer or platform orator could achieve was effected by the judges'.[4] The LRC promised to work with the TUC to reverse the judgement and, as many historians have noted, the embryonic Labour Party was rewarded with a substantial increase in membership, rising from more than 350,000 affiliated members in early 1901 to 861,000 in 1903.

At the same time, the LRC also began to build up its parliamentary representation. Hardie and Bell had been returned in 1900, although Bell proved to be a political renegade, seeing the LRC as a pressure group and supporting Liberal candidates in parliamentary by-elections before moving off towards the Liberal Party. Yet David Shackleton was returned, unopposed, in a by-election for Clitheroe in 1902, Will Crooks, for Woolwich, in March 1903, and Arthur Henderson, for Barnard Castle, in July 1903. The LRC had thus established a core of four reliable MPs by 1904. Hardie, the most established figure among them was to act as their chairman between 1903 and 1906 and was further endorsed as chairman of the Parliamentary Labour Party (PLP) in January 1906, when the number of LRC/Labour MPs was increased to twenty-nine, soon to be thirty with the switch of affiliation to them by one other MP.

What projected the LRC forward to its success in 1906 was the secret pact between the Liberal Chief Whip Herbert Gladstone and Ramsay MacDonald, in 1903, which secured for Labour, as it did for the Liberals, a straight run against the Conservatives in about thirty constituencies each. With the results of this arrangement becoming obvious in 1906, it became clear that the Liberal Party was no longer the party of the left, that it had once been. It was now faced with a serious challenge from the LRC, soon to be the Labour Party. The initial skirmish was led by James Keir Hardie, one of the great inspirational figures of the early Labour movement, who had been the first representative of independent Labour in the House of Commons in 1892 and, along with Ramsay MacDonald, Philip Snowden and J. Bruce Glasier, one of the 'Big Four' of the early Labour leaders. His early life and contribution to the Labour Party are worth exploring in detail.

JAMES KEIR HARDIE (1856–1915)

James Keir Hardie was once described as 'The most abused politician of his time. . . . No speaker had more meetings broken up in more continents than he.'[5] Returned as the first independent Labour MP in the House of Commons in 1892 he was dubbed the 'member for the unemployed' and the 'man in the cloth cap'. The idealist hero of the embryonic Labour Party, Hardie was associated with the ILP and the LRC/Labour Party and towered above all other leaders in the early years of the political Labour movement. Yet he proved to be something of a political loose cannon and acted as the unrestrained elder statesman of the Labour movement between 1907 and 1915. Unfairly, and inaccurately, John Burns once told him that he 'would be known as a leader who never won a strike, organized a Union, governed a parish or passed a Bill' and would be known as – 'Baron Cumnock in the Duchy of the Doctrinaire'.[6] In fact Hardie did organize a union, did pass a Bill and shaped the relatively speedy development of the early Labour Party.

Hardie was born in Lanarkshire, Scotland on 15 August 1856, the illegitimate son of a Scottish farm servant. He worked in a coal mine from the age of ten, was quickly involved in trade-union activities and moved to Cumnock, in Ayrshire, in the early 1880s, where he became deeply involved in Liberal politics. It was only the industrial and political conflicts in the 1880s that broke his allegiance to the Liberal Party. His outlook was changed further by the failure of the Scottish miners to develop effective trade unionism in 1886–7 and his activities as secretary of the Ayrshire Miners' Union. He set up and edited a newspaper, *The Miner*, established links with the socialists and unsuccessfully fought the Mid-Lanark parliamentary by-election in April 1888 as an independent Labour candidate. This campaign provided the platform for his successful efforts to form the Scottish Labour Party in August 1888. This organization brought together land reformers, trade unionists and radicals in the kind of broad alliance of interests which Hardie so favoured throughout his political life.

Hardie shot to fame as the founding father of independent Labour politics when he was returned to Parliament as the first independent Labour member for West Ham South in July 1892, having been selected by the West Ham South Radical Association (which included both radicals and socialists) as their candidate. From his parliamentary platform he attacked the Liberal government on labour questions.

It was not surprising that Hardie was asked to chair the meeting in January 1893 which saw the formation of the Independent Labour Party (ILP) at St George's Hall in Bradford. On that occasion he revealed his commitment to a flexibility of approach in dealing with electoral matters, challenging the attempt by Conference to impose a constitution; opposing the Manchester Fourth Clause, which would have committed ILP members and supporters to abstaining if there was no appropriate ILP candidate standing in an election; and stressing the need for 'each locality . . . be left to apply the Independence principle in its own way'.[7] Instead, he wished for fundamental principles, such as a commitment to socialism, to be agreed. Given his prominence within the independent Labour movement it is not surprising that he also acted as chairman (president 1894–6) of the ILP from 1893 to 1900. Hardie's position was further strengthened by the launch of the *Labour Leader*, the successor to *The Miner*, which became a weekly publication from March 1894. He owned and edited it until 1904 and it provided him with a journalistic and propagandizing base.

The great hope during the 1895 general election, was that since 'the Liberal party is shedding its members at both ends'[8] the ILP would pick up more parliamentary seats. That did not occur; Hardie lost his seat at West Ham South. Later, in November 1896, he contested, unsuccessfully, the Bradford East by-election. In this context, the future of the ILP was now open to question. Should it join with other socialist groups in forming a party of Socialist Unity or should it seek a broader alliance of socialists and trade unionists? Hardie decided upon the latter course, thwarting efforts to get the ILP and the SDF to join. Soon afterwards, in September 1900, Hardie was returned to Parliament for Merthyr, despite his open opposition to the Boer War. It was truly a remarkable success. Hardie represented that constituency until his death in 1915, maintaining a robust commitment to political independence but willing to do electoral deals with the Liberals; a constant, if somewhat contradictory, feature of his political outlook.

Nevertheless, he was the first person to put forward a motion in the House of Commons which demanded that Britain should form a 'Socialist Commonwealth founded upon the common ownership of land, capital, production use and not for profit, and equality for every citizen.' In other words, his socialist credentials were emerging.

Once in the House of Commons, Hardie, on his own initiative, deftly steered the LRC to agree to the formation of 'a distinct Labour group with their own Whip', that is to say to the formation of the Parliamentary Labour Party (PLP). Until this point the Labour members were effectively followers without leaders. Hardie seems to have been kept informed about the possible pact with the Liberals which MacDonald was brokering throughout 1903, although he always remained elusive on the question of alliances.[9]

The successes of the LRC/Labour Party, in 1906, meant that the PLP was now a more viable group than ever before and needed a prominent chairman prepared to undertake the enormously increased administrative burden that it entailed. Hardie's leadership was necessary given that 'Of the thirty Members at the General Election twenty-six [were] without experience of Parliamentary procedure.'[10] Hardie had the name, the experience and the prestige if not the aptitude for administration. Yet J. Bruce Glasier, one of Britain's leading socialists, tried to put him off contesting the post, writing that: 'You should not accept nomination for the chairmanship unless it unexpectedly happens that the feeling in favour for you doing so is *unanimous and enthusiastic – and hardly so even if it were so.*'

Glasier was clearly acting as a conduit for the frustrations of other leading figures in the Labour Party. Nevertheless, regardless of his advice, Hardie did contest the election, defeating David Shackleton by fifteen votes to fourteen, a victory which the *Labour Leader*, no longer in Hardie's hands, confirmed by stressing that he was the only man for the job and had a unique political record which even Ramsay MacDonald and Philip Snowden could not rival.[11]

Thus Hardie was officially made chairman of the PLP in 1906 and 1907. At first, with the newly expanded Labour Party in buoyant mood, Hardie seemed to be successful, securing the reversal of the Taff Vale Judgment through the Trades Dispute Bill, which he and David Shackleton promoted, thus securing trade unions' immunity from prosecution for financial losses incurred in a strike.

In the summer of 1906 MacDonald made the point that 'I voted for Hardie as chairman with much reluctance as I could not persuade myself that he could fill the place.'[12] On another occasion he added that 'we never know where to find him. The result is that we are coming to the objectionable habit of coming to decisions without him.'[13] Philip Snowden, an emerging Labour Leader, made much the same point about the unbusinesslike attitude and unreliability of Hardie.[14] Apart from his unwillingness to act as a party man, Hardie developed his own individual political interests with a passion which often cut across those of the

Labour Party. Most obviously he found himself at odds with the Party over the women's suffrage question. As a close friend of the Pankhursts, Hardie was drawn into the activities of the Women's Social and Political Union (WSPU).

The WSPU had been founded in 1903 and supported the idea of women being given voting rights on the same basis as men, 'the limited franchise', rather than complete enfranchisement which still seemed a distant prospect. Almost obsessional about the issue, and the imprisonment of suffragettes in 1906 and 1907, Hardie raised the 'limited franchise' issue at the Labour Party Conference in 1907. The Conference, held at Belfast, voted against the limited franchise by 605,000 to 268,000, suggesting that it was a retrograde step.[15] Delegates were not impressed by the fact that the WSPU had advised voters to elect the Conservative-Unionist rather than the Labour candidate at the recent Cockermouth parliamentary by-election. This rejection provoked Hardie, in his winding-up speech, to threaten that 'he would have to seriously consider whether he could remain a Member of the Parliamentary Party'.[16] Arthur Henderson saved the day by finding a formula allowing individual members of the PLP to vote as they wished on the 'limited franchise'.

There were other points of conflict as well, most obviously that concerning the right of the Conference to instruct the PLP on its parliamentary programme. The 1907 Labour Party Conference committed the National Executive and the PLP to joint discussions on this issue. From the start Hardie was opposed to action and also saw the resolution rejecting the 'limited franchise' for women, passed at this Conference, as an attempt to impose Conference decisions upon the PLP. In this respect, of course, Hardie expressed a view, endorsed by all chairmen and leaders of the Labour Party ever since, that Conference cannot dictate the policies of the PLP. Hardie's view was endorsed in a compromise resolution, by 642,000 votes to 252,000, that Conference resolutions were 'opinions only' and the implementation of them would be left to the PLP. It was a point which Hardie reiterated three years later when he argued that 'In the House of Commons, the members of the Party have to decide their own policy without interference from the Executive or any outside authority.'[17]

Evidently, the responsibilities of balanced and constant leadership did not seem to fit well with Hardie's propagandist instincts. It was thus a relief to many that, after a serious illness in the spring of 1907, Hardie decided upon a world tour. It was left to David Shackleton, vice-chairman of the PLP, to explain to Hardie the PLP's initial opposition to this tour and, ultimately, to stand in during his absence. While Hardie was away, the PLP elected Arthur Henderson as the new chairman in 1908.

Yet Hardie was quite defensive of the PLP on some matters. His personal animosity towards Ben Tillett, the famous trade-union leader, and leader of the London Dock Strike of 1889, positively encouraged him to criticize Tillett's pamphlet *Is the Parliamentary Labour Party a Failure* (1908) which claimed that 'The lion has no teeth or claws, and is losing his growl too; the temperance section being softly feline in their purring to Ministers and their patronage.'

Loyalty to Labour also led Hardie to exhort against Victor Grayson, who had been elected as MP for Colne Valley, Yorkshire in 1907. Grayson made two personal demonstrations in the House of Commons in October 1908. He was ejected because of his refusal to be bound by the rules of the House of Commons on the first occasion and, on the second, because he stated that 'This House is a House of murderers.' Hardie felt that Grayson's actions were premeditated and that he had been high-handed in failing to work with the PLP. This feud between Hardie and Grayson extended further when H.M. Hyndman, leader of the quasi-Marxist Social Democratic Federation, and Grayson refused to speak on the platform alongside Hardie at Holborn Town Hall in November 1908.

These were heady political times; David Lloyd George's People's Budget was being fought in the House of Commons and the House of Lords, while Hardie strongly supported the suggestion of 6*d* in the pound supertax on incomes above £5,000 per annum. The resistance of the Lords led Hardie to complain that the House of Lords was the 'cut of the tail of the mad dog'.

THE LABOUR PARTY 1906–14

The Labour Party that emerged in 1906 was essentially a reformist organization, dedicated to winning the support of the trade unions and temperamentally allied to the Liberal government. It was dominated by socialist leaders but was a party of independent labour, rather than socialism, since it needed to attract into it many trade-union members who were still essentially both Liberal and Conservative in political orientation. Although the Labour Party was influenced by the Fabians, who were committed to gradual social change by constitutional means, it was the ILP's ethical and moral brand of socialism that influenced its thinking and that of its supportive trade unions up to its clear acceptance of socialism in 1918.

The cultural and ethical approach of the ILP was vital to the development of the early Labour Party. It was a gut reaction to injustice and simply demanded reform. Ethical socialism was, indeed, an appeal to the heart rather than the mind. This is perhaps not surprising since Bruce Glasier, Philip Snowden, Keir Hardie and Ramsay MacDonald, the 'Big Four' of the ILP, the last three of whom were active in the Labour Party, held a moralistic approach to socialism which they carried into the Labour Party. They all revealed their Nonconformist and radical background and, with the exception of Snowden, their grounding in the Scottish land reform and nationalization movement. With all four it was the Liberal Radicalism of the past, and the desire for more democratic reforms, that influenced their thinking. Clearly, the ILP was shorn of any crude Marxist economic determinism, based upon relating class relations to the ownership of the means of production and the inevitability of class conflict in the process of bringing about revolutionary change. Yet to present the ILP and its influence upon the Labour Party simply in a moralistic framework is to ignore what both the ILP and the Labour Party were about.

In one respect they were concerned with the reorganization of society within an evolving community rather than one that was the product of class conflict. Ramsay MacDonald, a leading figure in both the ILP and the LRC/Labour Party before 1914, attempted to define his socialism in thirteen books written between 1905 and 1921, most of them produced by the National Labour Press, the ILP and the Socialist Library rather than commercial publishers.[18] These included *Socialism and Society* (1905), *Labour and Empire* (1906), *Socialism* (1907), *Socialism and Government* (2 vols, 1909), *Syndicalism* (1912), *Socialism after the War* (1917) and *Socialism: Critical and Constructive* (1921). These offered no clear body of integrated thought although they provided some clues to the policies of a future Labour government. For instance, *Labour and Empire* suggested that socialists would run the colonies indirectly, indicating MacDonald's Fabian upbringing in the suggestion of a superior and impartial force operating for the good of the colonies. Yet the dominant theme of these books was a form of social Darwinism. In the patchwork of ideas that appeared as *Socialism and Society* and *Socialism*, MacDonald rejected the competitive struggle for existence as the chief characteristic of social evolution in favour of the increasing tendency towards cooperation. He emphasized that economic development was the mainspring of change but that man's reasoning gave shape and direction to the demands for change. Yet there could be no appeal to narrow class interests, for society had to be run for the good of the community as a whole. This was an eclectic set of ideas which drew from Marxist economic determinism and the moral ideals of the ethical socialists but above all reaffirmed the Fabian belief that the central socialist goal of public ownership could be achieved through the gradual modification of existing institutions. The idea of the impartial role of the state arose from the fact that, to MacDonald, 'Socialism is no class movement. Socialism is a movement of opinion, not an organisation of status. It is not the rule of the working class; it is the organisation of the community.'[19] In other words, socialism would develop as society evolved and became more enlightened, and not as a result of the development of class conflict and the rise of the working class.

At the same time as MacDonald was giving the impression that the ILP aimed for a society of all the classes, not simply of the working class, Keir Hardie, the only one of the Labour and ILP 'big four' who had trade-union credentials, was moving the ILP and the Labour Party towards strengthening the links with trade unionism. Evidently, the Labour Party was becoming the party of class just as its main leaders were claiming to represent the interests of all classes.

This situation had been encouraged by the Taff Vale Case but became clearer when the Liberal Party was reluctant to become involved in protecting the interests of trade unions. It is true that the Liberal government's Trades Dispute Act of 1906 nullified the Taff Vale Judgment but it came too late to staunch the flow of trade-union support from the Liberal Party to the Labour Party. The outburst of industrial conflict between 1910 and 1914, which produced national transport and mining strikes, strengthened and speeded up the process of rising trade-union support for the Labour Party despite the counter-claims of support made by a small group of syndicalists led by Tom Mann, a British socialist of international stature who was demanding that workers form themselves into one union within each industry *en route* to forming a parliament of such unions in order to call a general strike to bring about the downfall of capitalism.

There is also convincing evidence that the Liberal Party could not cope with the demands of trade unions.[20] A significant proportion of the TUC membership, and particularly the coal mining unions, who had Lib-Lab MPs (working-class MPs connected with the Liberal Party), retained their Liberal connections up to 1908. Indeed, many trade unionists were still suspicious of socialists and both the Liberal and Conservative parties vied for their support despite the fact that many trade unions paid political funds to Labour. But the Osborne Judgment put the matter beyond doubt.

Walter Osborne, a Conservative member of the Amalgamated Society of Railway Servants, was determinedly opposed to the Labour Party and extolled the virtues of trade unionism coming to an accommodation with capital, in order to achieve industrial harmony, increased output and improved wages. What he objected to was the socialist type of trade unionism which had emerged to advocate state intervention and the eight-hour day. On an individual basis he campaigned against individual members of trade unions being asked to contribute to the political funds of the Labour Party and used the law to uphold his objection in 1908 and 1909. He took legal action to prevent the ASRS from levying funds for the Labour Party and was supported by the House of Lords. This decision created problems for both the Liberal and Unionist parties. The trade unionists wished for a reversal of the judgment and the Liberals in particular were torn between resisting an action which could lead to the strengthening of ties between the trade unions and the Labour Party and presenting too hostile a reaction that would alienate trade unionists.

Both Conservative-Unionists and Liberals were in a quandary and this was reflected by the split within the Liberal Party. While Herbert Samuel, a Liberal MP, detected that if the Osborne Judgment was not reversed then the result would be 'to increase the separation between labour and Liberalism', Sir William Robson, a Liberal Attorney General, felt that the conflict between the Liberals and socialists was inevitable: 'Nothing can avoid this conflict. It is also unfortunately too clear that the Socialists are in effective command of the Trade Union organization, and if they are at liberty to draw on that organization for funds they may do so up to £80,000 or £100,000 per annum. . . .'[21] To Robson, there was still a majority of trade unionists who objected to the political fund, although this was due to their 'inert assent'.

David Lloyd George entered into secret negotiations with the Unionists to block a reversal of the Osborne Judgment, so the 1913 Trade Union Act did not reverse the judgment but, rather, permitted unions to hold a secret ballot on the issue. The fact is that neither the Liberal nor the Unionist parties felt much compunction to change the Osborne

Judgment. In the end it rebounded upon them as union after union, holding secret ballots under the Trade Union Act, voted in favour of Labour representation. By the beginning of 1914 about 420,000 trade unionists, from unions with a membership of 1,208,841, had voted on the necessity of establishing political funds for the Labour Party. Of these, 298,702 voted in favour and 125,310 against.[22] The organized trade-union movement and its active rank and file were overwhelmingly committed to the Labour Party before the onset of war. Indeed, 'These votes ensured Labour's post-First World War electoral finances, and in themselves reflect an element of the explanation for the rise of the Labour Party and the decline of the Liberal Party in the early twentieth century.'[23]

The Labour Party's political strength was increased after 1906 by the affiliation of more trade unions, and particularly the Miners' Federation of Great Britain on 1 January 1909, and the switch of allegiance of their MPs from the Liberal Party to the Labour Party. In the January 1910 general election Labour won 40 seats from 78 contests and in the December 1910 general election won 42 from 56 contests. This was down on Labour's position in 1909, and it lost 6 seats in by-elections between 1911 and 1914. It was down to 37 MPs by 1914. Nevertheless, despite these election setbacks, Labour's parliamentary achievements were remarkably good given that 6 million men and many more millions of women, a substantial proportion of whom would have voted Labour, did not have the vote.

Indeed, the increasing political power of the Labour Party and the ILP can be seen by the tremendous surge in municipal success from 1909 onwards and the vast increase in other local successes, for instance in boards of guardians, urban district councils, rural district councils, parish councils, and other local public bodies. These changes have remained largely unexamined except for one detailed study of the textile district of the West Riding of Yorkshire.[24] Labour's municipal victories in England and Wales rose from 82 in 1909 to 171 in 1913 and about 500 of the 8,000 municipal seats were held by Labour on the eve of war. In addition there were other significant signs of growth, for the Labour Party had increased the number of its MPs from two in 1900 to thirty in 1906 and forty-two in December 1910.

Women also played an integral part in Labour's early growth. Many working-class women were drawn into both the activities of the Labour Party and the women's suffrage campaign and there was a fluid, if sometimes conflicting relationship, between the various women's and labour/socialist organizations.[25] The Women's Labour League was the only autonomous group of women that has ever existed within the Labour Party. Its history has been obscured, largely because of the male-dominated nature of the political movement and because it was strongly middle class, but it was a body that sought to be a sister organization to the LRC set up 'by women for women'. At its first conference in 1906, an amendment from Isabella Ford, a Leeds socialist and feminist, was accepted stating that one of the organization's aims was to 'obtain direct representation in Parliament and on local bodies'. Thus from the very beginning the League was committed to the idea of women's suffrage despite the Labour Party's ambivalence on this issue at the time, and was therefore a credible organization in the eyes of the contemporary women's movement.[26] It was not, however, a totally independent body for it sought affiliation to the Labour Party from its inception and gained it during the First World War.[27] Its initial intention was also to establish the importance of an agenda of political issues that affected the lives of women. At its Annual Conference of 1913, the view was expressed that 'We may say that much of the attention given in late years to the condition of children is our work. We have . . . directed attention to the need of feeding in the schools . . . we have spoken and agitated about the medical needs of children.'[28] Evidently, its aim was to give 'a channel for the special knowledge and experiences of women of the party'.[29]

The Labour Party's political actions were remarkable, despite the criticisms from socialist critics. In 1907 and 1908 it introduced the Unemployed Workmen's Bill and campaigned for the right to work and to establish that local authorities should provide work or adequate maintenance. It had also forced the Liberal government to pass the Trade Union Act of 1913, and pressed for and got the payment of MPs in 1913, which greatly improved the financial position of the Party. There is no doubt that it could have done more but the very fact that the Labour Party and the ILP had secured the majority of trade-union support by 1914, and were winning significant local and parliamentary political victories, are achievements that should not be slighted given the prevailing political climate of the Edwardian years when Labour was competing with a reforming Liberal administration. It would have been easy for the Labour Party to have become subsumed within progressivism, but in effect its connections with the trade unions cut across the aspirations of the New Liberalism, the emphasis upon social harmony that was developing within the Liberal Party.

WHY DID LABOUR RISE? CLASS POLITICS OR ACCIDENTS OF WAR?

Clearly, the years between 1906 and the end of the First World War saw a fundamental change in the balance of political power, particularly within the progressive politics of Britain. The general election of 1905/6 brought the Liberal Party back to office with 400 MPs, after a period of eleven years in opposition. Although the Conservative-Unionist Party was still the second largest parliamentary party, it had been defeated and the real political danger to the Liberal Party lay in the fact that the Labour Representation Committee, soon to be the Labour Party, had returned thirty MPs, thus enormously increasing its pre-election strength among the progressive electorate. This development, more than the subsequent revival of the Conservative Party, was to be the dominating political theme of these years and the cause of much contemporary and current debate.

The major events of Labour growth and Liberal decline have been outlined. Labour supported the Liberal administration, became increasingly important in that respect after the 1910 general elections and, in May 1915, was drawn into the wartime Coalition government. It obviously looked well positioned to assume the mantle of the progressive party in British politics at the end of the war when the Liberal Party was divided and when Lloyd George's government was only sustained by the Conservative Party.

Yet, the Liberal Party had seemed omnipotent in 1906. It had achieved a landslide victory in the general election of December 1905/January 1906 and was intending to build up its political support among the working classes by offering social reforms which were more intrusive than any they had offered before, and which sought to tackle some of the major social problems of unemployment, ill health, old age and poverty. Social harmony was its objective but also both its perceived strength and weakness. While social reform did help to attract working-class support in some areas and kept the Labour Party on its side this philosophy also meant that it sought not to choose sides in an industrial dispute. The lack of New Liberal support for trade unions in disputes thus led to a reaffirmation of trade-union commitment to the emergent Labour Party. The First World War further weakened the Liberal Party by raising issues of policy and leadership which divided rather than united it. The Liberal shibboleths of peace, retrenchment and free trade were all challenged and undermined by the war, there were Liberal doubts about the formation of the Coalition government and some disquiet on the conduct of the war, which saw Lloyd George replace H.H. Asquith as Prime Minister in December 1916. In the end, it was a divided Liberal Party that fought the general election of December 1918. As a result, the Party under Asquith declined to a rump of MPs while the Liberal Party under Lloyd George helped to form a Coalition government with the dominating and overwhelming support of the Conservative-Unionist Party.

The rise of Labour and the decline of the Liberal Party have been the subject of bitter and intense debate for the last sixty years or so. The main cause of Liberal decline and Labour growth is obvious: the voters had deserted the Liberal Party in favour of its Labour and Conservative rivals. Yet why should many voters abandon a lifelong commitment to the Liberal Party? Several major reasons have been given for this. Clearly, Labour's growth was rapid before 1914 largely because it had captured the trade unions, and thus working-class support from the Liberal Party, as already suggested. Nevertheless, there were immense variations in this trend from region to region and from town to town which were firmly 'rooted in local political and economic conflict and the corresponding decline in working-class Liberal support'.[30] For instance, whereas Bradford saw the rapid growth of the Labour Party before 1914 it is clear that Huddersfield retained a strong Liberal presence and tradition, particularly at the local level, as late as the early 1960s – although this was largely because the Liberal Party operated an effective anti-socialist alliance with the Conservatives.[31] It is also possible that the Liberal Party declined rapidly as a result of the First World War which saw the split in the Liberal Party between Asquith and Lloyd George. In any case, the First World War clearly challenged the old Liberal values.

Some of these are clearly rival explanations which have attracted the attention of many historians and led to heated debate over the last sixty years – ever since the Liberal Party splintered and practically faded away altogether in the 1930s. The detailed analysis of these debates, and sub-debates, is examined elsewhere, and focuses upon whether or not the Labour Party had won significant working-class support before 1914, and had thus become a party of class interest, or whether the First World War, in dividing the Liberal Party, was the main reason for Labour's growth.[32] Sub-debates have also developed around the extent to which the franchise, New Liberalism and the variation of local conditions affected events. However, it is clear that there is an immense variation of evidence and that the patchwork of experience is not open to easy interpretation. In fact, no one interpretation has yet become dominant.

Recent attempts to examine development have, however, shed fresh light on what was occurring. Indeed, there have been two important studies. David Howell's book on the *British Workers and the Independent Labour Party 1888–1906* (Manchester University Press, 1984) surveyed the main ILP areas and acknowledged that the ILP and Labour Party support was patchy. Yet far more controversial has been Duncan Tanner's book, *Political Change and the Labour Party* (Cambridge University Press, 1991) which concludes that by 1914 there was an uneven pattern of political control between Labour and the Liberals, although he argues that Labour support 'was comparatively strong where Liberal Party support was weak and unable to seriously rival it in more Liberal areas. Cooperation was therefore possible.'[33] In the end, he maintains, Labour was not posed to replace the Liberal Party in 1914 and Labour had no generally successful area of support.

A BALANCED APPROACH TO THE RISE OF THE LABOUR PARTY

Clearly a more balanced approach is necessary which accepts that the First World War was responsible for significant political and social change but admits that the Liberal Party was finding great difficulty in containing Labour's pre-war challenge. The Liberal Party's problems were largely a product of its own inability to absorb the organized working class within its political structure. In the end, the lack of a positive response from the Liberal Party drove working men to look towards the Labour Party not for socialism so much as for the representation of their own sectional interests.

Indeed, the crunch question is at what point did the working class transfer their allegiance from the Liberal Party to the Labour Party? The balance of evidence suggests that this occurred before 1914 and via the trade-union movement. In part, the reason for this would appear to be the unwillingness of the local Liberal parties to permit working-class candidates to stand as Liberals in the local and the parliamentary elections. What the national Liberal Party and its local organizations failed to appreciate was the seething discontent at this rejection which had erupted among trade unionists from the mid-1880s onwards, when in towns such as Bradford Liberal trade unionists like Samuel Shaftoe, were continuously rejected in their attempts to become Liberal candidates for the municipal councils. This neglect of working-class interests by the Liberals combined with working-class anger and frustration to produce an independent Labour movement.

Few historians doubt the importance of industrial conflict in creating the climate of independent political action by the working classes. E.P. Thompson, the famous socialist historian, noted this and even many of the sceptics of Labour's pre-war political growth concur.[34] The strikes among the girls at the Bryant and May match factory in 1888, among the London dockers of 1889, the gasworkers in 1889 and 1890 and the textile workers of the Manningham Mills strike of 1890–1 have thus attracted the attention of historians who have seen them as uniting skilled, semi-skilled and unskilled workers into an economic conflict with their employers which had political implications. In fact, the Manningham Mills strike had immense political importance in Bradford, and the textile area of the West Riding, for 'the struggle took on the character of a general dispute between capital and labour'[35] and 'Labour had so associated itself that even defeat must be victory'.[36] Indeed, the wider Labour movement identified with the several thousand Manningham strikers and paved the way for the formation of the Bradford Labour Union, the embryonic Bradford Independent Labour Party, in May 1891.

In the wake of such events local Labour unions and Independent Labour parties were formed, leading to the formation of the national Independent Labour Party in January 1893. Within seven years, following the disastrous general election performance in 1895, the ILP had pushed for the formation of the LRC in 1900.

The formation of the LRC was seen as an affirmation of the alliance with trade unions and the capture of the support of the Miners' Federation of Great Britain in May 1908, leading to its affiliation in January 1909, confirmed the success of the Labour Party's attempt to widen its trade-union support. Yet how much of this support was genuinely committed to the Party, given that political allegiances are difficult to break?[37] There is much evidence to suggest that once the Labour Party came into existence it offered an alternative focus of activity. The emergence of a loosely based Lib-Lab arrangement in Edwardian politics distanced the Liberal Party from the trade unions, since trade-union influence was to be increasingly directed through the Labour Party. The very formulation of the Lib-Lab pact in 1903 was anathema to the New Liberal idea of a harmony of interests operating within the Liberal Party. Above all, it was rapidly becoming clear that the Liberal Party could not embrace trade unionism after 1900 and that by 1914 British trade unionism was firmly identified with the Labour Party. This meant that the Labour Party became politically viable and that the Liberal Party had lost political support. This development helped to ensure that the Fabian Society, which had affiliated with the LRC/Labour Party in 1900 but had still sought to work closely with the Liberals, particularly in London, would be pinning its colours to Labour's political mast by the beginning of the First World War.

CONCLUSION

The rise of Labour and the decline of Liberalism are events which are not easily explained. The rise of class politics, as evidenced through the increasing trade-union support of Labour and local organic developments, was just as much a factor in the transformation of progressive politics in Britain as was the First World War. The problem is one of assessing the point at which the process of change became inexorable. In this respect, it is clear that the process of political change was well established before the First World War. Local research combines with national evidence to suggest that a powerful Labour Party had emerged with MPs, rising trade-union membership and increasing financial support. In addition, Old Liberalism, which was unresponsive to the demands for direct working-class representation, remained the dominant strand in most regions throughout the country. Only in areas where the Liberal Party needed to change in order to increase its political support was there much evidence of a New Liberal presence, and even there its influence may have been impaired by the obvious equivocation of its leaders towards reversing the Osborne Judgment in case that action should further encourage the growth of the Labour Party. The fact is that the Labour Party was a significant political party on the eve of the First World War, though it obviously under-performed in parliamentary elections because of the difficulties of the pre-war franchise. How much difference the 1918 franchise made is still open to speculation but there is no doubt that Labour was making significant progress in local elections and in some parliamentary by-elections between 1910 and 1914.

In 1914 the Labour Party was well established and threatening the dominance of the Liberal Party in progressive politics, a process which was undoubtedly speeded up by the Asquith–Lloyd George split of 1916. It is difficult to believe, given the pre-war developments, that the First World War was solely responsible for the decline of the Liberal Party or, conversely, that it came 'just in time to save the Labour Alliance'.[38] Nevertheless, the First World War did speed up the process of political change in British society which had been brought by the emergence of class politics before 1914.

CHAPTER TWO

Labour at War, 1914–18

The First World War exerted a major impact upon the British Labour Party. It contributed to the growth of state intervention, divided the Liberals, directed the progressive vote to Labour, and amplified the link between the Labour Party and British trade unionism. It may have even weakened and fragmented socialism in Britain. In the specific context of the Labour Party the First World War saw three major developments. It reduced the influence of the Independent Labour Party, over the Labour Party, thus confirming the dominance of the trade-union movement. The ILP, the intellectual godparent of the Labour Party declined in influence because it opposed the war and also because the Labour Party had adopted a socialist constitution. More importantly, the war saw the Labour Party produce a new constitution, in 1918, which committed it to the public ownership of the means of production – the famous Clause Four. The importance of this particular event has divided historians between those who feel that this was a conscious decision, arrived at after the sifting of socialist alternatives within the context of war, and those who feel that it was an afterthought which carried little significance and deflected attention from the fact that right-wing trade unionism was strengthened within the Labour Party by the 1918 Constitution. It is possible that there was more continuity in Labour politics than is supposed and that Clause Four, at that time, carried less influence than is often claimed. Also, as already proposed in the previous chapter, it is possible that the war paved the way for Labour's growth by either galvanizing the class politics it had already established or by dividing the Liberal Party and creating a gap in progressive politics into which the Labour Party could slip.

LABOUR AND THE WAR

When war broke out in August 1914 it exerted an immediate impact upon the objectives of the Labour Party. On the eve of war the Labour leaders, and a good proportion of the Labour Party throughout the country, were opposed to conflict and prepared to fight militarism. There was widespread support for the idea of a 'general stoppage of work' in Britain to coincide with similar anti-war actions in other countries. One writer, in the Labour paper *The Bradford Pioneer*, noted that

> Alone amongst the parties of Britain the Labour Party is pledged against militarism. . . . We must take up the 'Fiery Cross' and carry it to the remotest hamlet in the country, call every man and woman to the colours, 'Down with militarism'. That is our cry – as it is also the cry of our comrades all over Europe. Blazon it on the banners. Write it on the pavement. Sing it in the streets.[1]

Yet the outbreak of the First World War came with startling suddenness and the Labour opposition was submerged by the rising wave of nationalism. Very quickly, the great majority of the Labour Party pledged themselves to support the war effort, although there was some significant opposition from the likes of James Ramsay MacDonald, who resigned from the chairmanship of the Parliamentary Labour Party in 1914, and from the leadership, if not necessarily the rank and file, of the Independent Labour Party, who were opposed to the war. The Labour Party agreed to the political truce for the duration of the war and eventually joined in the two Coalition governments, formed under H.H. Asquith in May 1915 and David Lloyd George in December 1916. The Trades Union Congress (TUC) also supported such fusion politics by declaring an industrial truce and accepting the Munitions Act, which outlawed strikes in connection with war work, in 1915.

Thus the war had deflected the Labour Party from its intended path. Patriotism replaced peace and the formal arrangement of Coalition government replaced the informal association of the Labour and Liberal parties that had dominated the politics of the immediate pre-war years. Indeed, leading Labour figures, such as Arthur Henderson and George N. Barnes, became prominent members in the Coalition governments. However, this commitment did create tensions. The introduction of military conscription in January 1916 produced dissent within the Labour Party and the wider Labour movement. Arthur Henderson, Labour's leader, resigned as Leader of the House of Commons and from the War Cabinet in August 1917, when Labour leaders were refused permission to attend an international socialist conference to discuss peace. But he was replaced and Labour remained part of the wartime Coalition government.

The war had an immediate and profound impact upon the position of labour. There was now an increasing demand for workers, wage levels rose quickly and trade-union membership increased rapidly. Indeed, there were 2,565,000 trade unionists in 1910, 4,145,000 in 1914 and 6,533,000 in 1918. The figure had risen to well over 8 million by 1920. This growth, in turn, improved the financial situation of the Labour Party, which was now the beneficiary of an increasing amount of trade-union funding. Not surprisingly, when the Labour Party Constitution of 1918 was introduced, it was the trade unions who were the most obvious beneficiaries. Thirteen of the twenty-three members of the National Executive Committee (NEC) were automatically trade unionists, and the other ten, representing women, socialists and the rest of the Party interests, were voted upon by the trade unionists. Clause Four, the socialist commitment to public ownership, plus the creation of individual membership arrangements, might have attracted the headlines but the blunt fact was that it was the trade unions, not the socialists, who benefited from Labour's 1918 Constitution. In this respect, the war strengthened the hand of trade unionism.

It also meant that the membership of the Labour Party, entirely institutional until the 1918 Constitution was introduced, increased. Indeed, Labour Party membership rose from 2,100,000 in 1915 to 3,500,000 by the beginning of 1919.

The First World War also saw the introduction of the Representation Act of 1918, although its introduction had been trailed well before 1914. This gave the parliamentary vote to all men over twenty-one years of age, apart from peers, and to all women above the age of thirty. With manhood and part womanhood suffrage, which abandoned the old system based upon property, the electorate expanded from around 7 million to about 21 million, including millions of working-class voters. Even in the politically inert atmosphere of the political truce all the major wartime political parties had to adapt, especially since the electoral boundaries and constituencies had also been changed.

The Labour Party responded by increasing the number of constituency organizations. There were 215 divisional parties and trades councils affiliated to Labour in January 1918, 397 by June 1918 and 400 in 1919. These organizations were the unified constituency parties that were to replace the free-for-all of competing labour interests that had previously selected parliamentary candidates. They brought a greater sense of unity within the Labour Party, and particularly within constituencies.

Despite some divisions and tensions the Labour Party did well out of the war. Its membership had increased and it had gained experience in government. However, it is upon two areas, the emergence of Clause Four and the development of class politics, already discussed in Chapter One, that most debate has been focused.

THE LABOUR PARTY AND CLAUSE FOUR

The main question has been: did the war bring about fundamental change within Labour or simply extend and perpetuate existing trends? This is central to the debate about Clause Four, which made the Labour Party a socialist body for the first time.

The origins and importance of Clause Four have been debated by contemporaries and modern historians. It was put into sharp focus in 1974 with the publication of J.M. Winter's *Socialism and the Challenge of War: Ideas and Politics in Britain, 1912–18* and R. McKibbin's *The Evolution of the Labour Party 1910–1924*, two books which disagreed over whether or not Clause Four should be taken seriously as a statement of Labour's socialism.[2]

It was Winter who developed the orthodox view that the First World War brought about significant changes in British society. Winter argued that the improved incomes and employment prospects of all workers resulted in the blurring of distinctions within the working class and between classes. He argued that the deep involvement of all sections of society in the war effort led to a decline in the deferential attitudes of the working class and the rising prospect of political and social change. In this environment, Labour leaders were forced to conclude that the restructuring of the Labour Party was essential and they were forced to sift through a variety of socialist policies in order to select those which would be most apposite to its postwar growth. In the final analysis, then, the wartime conditions favoured the collectivist (or state ownership) policies of Beatrice and Sidney Webb, the prominent Fabians, and paved the way for the 1918 Labour Constitution and Clause Four, and then the Party's clear commitment to a future socialist state.

Such an interpretation, suggesting a change in the pattern of Labour's development, is entirely alien to Ross McKibbin, who rejects the view that the wartime economy made much difference to the potential of Labour politics. He cannot believe that the men who drew up the new Labour Constitution, most of whom were in their fifties and sixties, were capable of dramatic conversion or that Clause Four was anything other than an 'uncharacteristic adornment' of the new Constitution. To him, the trends in British Labour development were evident before the war and Clause Four was simply a response to the wider electorate which was to be created by the Representation of the People Act of 1918. He believes that it is inconceivable that it could have been otherwise, given that the Labour Party was moving to the right not the left, during the war, a fact evidenced by the increased trade-union control of the National Executive Committee of the Labour Party under the 1918 Labour Constitution.[3]

There are clearly many differences of emphasis but the major issue is that of the difference between socialism and Labour interests. While Winter sees the Labour Party moving towards accepting a socialism based upon state control McKibbin feels that it was Labour interests and the balance of power, which allowed for trade-union control of the Party, that was vital to the reshaped Labour Party.

The role of the War Emergency Committee is obviously vital to Winter's argument, if not to that of McKibbin.[4] It was drawn together on 5 August 1914 after Arthur Henderson, Secretary of the Labour Party, had written to the NEC to call a special meeting 'to consider what action should be taken in the very serious crisis in Europe and any other business that may arise'.[5] It was formed in the context of a Labour Party committed to peace but within a day it was being called to act for a movement which was committed to the war effort. Its prime function became the defence of the rights and interests of the working class from unreasonable encroachment. It quickly evolved to include the Co-operative Union and the Co-operative Wholesale Society. Its policy of co-option also led to invitations to Ramsay MacDonald and several hundred individuals to join it, and the absorption of the representatives of many trade unions, the ILP, the British Socialist Party, the National Socialist Party, the Fabian Society and many other organizations. In short, it was the most representative body in the British Labour movement, incorporating both pro-war and anti-war organizations.[6]

The primary objective of the War Emergency Committee (WEC) was to keep the Labour movement from disintegrating under the impact of war. To achieve this end, the WEC concentrated its efforts on assuming a leading role in defending the living standard of the population. It protested at the 70 per cent inflation that occurred between 1914 and 1916, worked for rent restriction in 1915 and to ensure that there was an adequate distribution of food supplies.

Towards the end of the war, however, the WEC became far more positive in its policies and more aggressive in its approach. The introduction of compulsory military service in 1916 brought about a fundamental change in its strategy. It protested against the Military Service Act in 1916 and developed a campaign for the 'Conscription of Riches' as a *quid pro quo* for Labour's contribution to providing manpower for the trenches. The WEC's policy was the 'Conscription of Wealth', through income tax, supertax, capital tax and sequestration of all unearned income, and the nationalization of all industries then under government control for the duration of the war.[7]

Why did the Labour Party commit itself to the socialist goal? Was it because of the growth of Webbian socialism, with its belief in state control, thrust forward by the First World War and through the WEC, or was it simply a product of political expediency?

There is no doubting that the socialist ideas of the Webbs were attractive to some sections of the Labour movement. The ILP and the Fabians had already declared their commitment to both vague and broad resolutions connected with the common ownership of the means of production. It is also possible that the Russian revolutions of 1917, and particularly the Bolshevik Revolution which occurred soon after Arthur Henderson's ill-fated trip to Russia in 1917, forced Labour leaders to adopt a resolution that would offer a less violent and a more democratic way to socialism. There is also the suggestion that the professional middle classes were being drawn to such a policy in the wake of the government collectivization policy. In addition, the Lloyd George Coalition government set up a Ministry of Reconstruction to prepare policies for the postwar years. Of the nine members of the central Advisory Council attached to the ministry two, Ernest Bevin and J.H. Thomas, were trade unionists and active members of the Labour Party. Apart from being in the Coalition, Labour was being drawn into efforts to prepare schemes for housing, health and social welfare policies on a broader front in the postwar years. It must have appeared that old *laissez-faire* capitalism was dead and that socialist policies, particularly the state socialist ones of the Webbs, were now more relevant than ever. Many Labour activists would have found it hard to imagine that the wartime collectivism would be dismantled, especially after the formation of the Ministry of Reconstruction.

Clause Four (or Party Object 'd') ran as follows:

To secure for producers by hand or by brain the full fruits of their industry, and the most equitable distribution thereof that may be possible, upon the basis by the Common Ownership of the Means of Production and the best obtainable system of popular administration and control of each industry and service.

It was a very imprecise statement of socialist intent. Ross McKibbin suggests, as already noted, that it was an 'uncharacteristic adornment' of the new Constitution of the Labour Party not meant to be taken seriously. That may be so, but presumably it meant something to someone. If it is assumed that it was useful in order to distinguish the Labour Party from the Liberal Party, to indicate Labour's political independence, then it is fair to assume that this socialist ideology was important to some sections of the Labour Party and its supporters.

It is possible that the vagueness of Clause Four permitted it to act as a unifying force within the Labour Party. The various labour and socialist organizations which accreted to the Labour Party exhibited widely different views about socialism and war. Some organizations favoured a type of workers' control while others wished for an extensive programme of nationalization. Many organizations were pro-war but some, like the Independent Labour Party and the British Socialist Party, after 1916, associated with the Peace Campaign of 1917 and were represented at the Workers' and Soldiers' Conference at Leeds, organized to give moral support to the Russian Revolution of February/March 1917. The WEC managed to unite these interests through the defence of living standards and via its 'Conscription of Riches' campaign. Clause Four could be seen as an extension of this approach. Indeed, it has been suggested that

It [Clause Four] is better regarded as a rallying point around which the adherents of different ideologies and representatives of different interests assembled. . . . The adoption of Clause Four did not imply that the whole membership came to have a common objective, but rather that an objective had been proclaimed which both accommodated and concealed a large diversity of particular concerns.[8]

It was detailed enough to distinguish Labour men from the Liberal Party but sufficiently vague to avoid serious conflict over the variety of socialist programmes on offer.

Indeed, there is little evidence that Clause Four excited much interest at either the national or local level, beyond the recognition of the fact that, by accepting it, the Labour Party had formally declared its commitment to socialism. In West Yorkshire it was other issues, such as war and the protection of the standards of living of the working classes, that attracted most concern.[9] In the end, Clause Four proved a useful point of common agreement between socialists of all shades of opinion but it should not be seen as more than an acceptable flag of convenience which helped to detach the Labour Party from the progressive section of the Liberal Party.

CONCLUSION

What, then, are we to make of the impact of the First World War upon the Labour Party? The most obvious point is that the Labour Party had made important strides in developing it as the party of the working class before 1914. The First World War developed this trend further by strengthening the trade-union movement, and thus the Labour Party. In that sense the growth of the Labour Party ran along well-established grooves and, in most ways, was not a product of a dramatic change in direction produced by the war. Nevertheless, there is no doubt that the Labour Party did well out of the divisions within the Liberal Party, mentioned in the previous chapter, and Clause Four did unite the wider Labour movement in the common cause, socialism, even if that cause may have been peripheral to the interests of the increasingly trade-union dominated Labour Party.

CHAPTER THREE

Ramsay MacDonald and the Rise and Fall of the Labour Party, 1918–31

The Labour Party grew dramatically between 1918 and 1929, before collapsing, temporarily, in the October 1931 general election following Ramsay MacDonald's abandonment of the second Labour government and the formation of the National government in August 1931. Indeed, until 1931 the Labour Party had gone from strength to strength. With 23.7 per cent of the vote in the 1918 general election the Labour Party had secured 57 seats, 61 with subsequent additions on the opening of Parliament. In the 1929 general election it obtained 37.9 per cent of the vote, and 291 seats. The 1931 'MacDonald fiasco' reduced it to 31.2 per cent of the vote and a mere 52 MPs. Yet, despite this roller-coaster of a political ride, the Labour Party had clearly established itself as the second party of British politics seeing off the challenge of the Liberal Party. The Labour leadership may have deserted it in 1931 but the working-class vote remained remarkably resilient for the Labour Party throughout the interwar years and recovered quickly in the 1930s.

Several major features of Labour's development can be detected between 1918 and 1931 (see Chapter Two). The Labour Party had replaced the Liberal Party as the progressive party of British politics, although Labour was still faced with a substantial Liberal challenge, divided as the Liberals were, until the general election of 1924 when the Liberal Party was reduced to a mere forty MPs.[1] Despite the critical comment of some writers, it is also clear that the Labour Party had improved its organization and captured the working-class vote.[2] Certainly Ramsay MacDonald's political defection had done much damage to the Labour Party, although there is little evidence to suggest that his actions were part of some grand design. Indeed, the evidence

31

suggests that the economic conditions drove MacDonald to switch governments.[3]

Of these, the most dramatic development of the interwar years was the replacement of the Liberal Party by the Labour Party as the second party in British politics. In 1918 the Liberal Party, though divided, was still the second parliamentary party in Britain. However, in 1922, and again in 1923, the Liberal Party had been dramatically overtaken by the Labour Party, although it did stage a minor recovery in 1929. In contrast, the Labour Party's growth appeared almost inexorable. There had been a considerable change in progressive politics in Britain. While the late Henry Pelling, one of the leading historians of British Labour history, and many others, have stressed that emergence of trade-union support for the Labour Party ensured that it captured the working-class vote, more recent contributors have argued either that Labour came through to replace the Liberal Party because of its split in 1916 or that even then there was still a prospect that the Liberal Party could maintain its control of the progressive vote.[4] In fact the debate has moved on from that point with more recent contributors stressing the need to examine communities and regions in more detail.[5] For the interwar years, however, the main issue is how far had the degeneration of the Liberal Party gone and how deep-rooted was Labour's trade-union and working-class support. The issue is one of potential, for in 1918 the Liberals, divided between the supporters of Asquith and the supporters of Lloyd George, returned more MPs than the burgeoning Labour Party which faced the Coalition government of David Lloyd George. In this respect it is the second development, the extent and reason for Labour's growth, that has more direct relevance to the 1920s.

Christopher Howard has questioned the effectiveness of Labour's organization in the 1920s: 'The image of a vibrant expanding new party was an illusion. Labour was fortunate that its opponents were deceived.'[6] Yet labour leaders would not have agreed with this assessment, even though the title of Howard's article, 'Expectation born to death' is drawn from MacDonald's comment, written in 1921, that 'the Labour party knocks the heart out of me and expectations are like babies born to death'.[7]

Exactly why the Labour Party grew so rapidly in the decade after the First World War has been a matter of considerable argument between those advocating the long-term increase of working-class support for the Labour Party and those stressing the division of the Liberal Party during the First World War. Almost unwittingly, Howard accepts the first of these arguments for he notes that 'Widespread electoral support bore little resemblance to restricted party membership, however, and disappointments were common.'[8] Such a gap between organization and support could only be explained by class voting which took no note of party activity, if Howard's assumption of the weakness of Labour's political action is correct. But the issue is confused by the fact that Howard also asserts that both the Liberals and Conservatives would have been more successful had they seen through the illusion and perceived the real weakness of the Labour Party's organization. Howard does not appear to have made his mind up whether it was class politics or the illusion of a rapidly expanding Labour Party that accounts for Labour's electoral successes in the 1920s. He does not even consider the difficulties of a Liberal Party whose support was being squeezed both from the left and the right.

Nevertheless, the crux of Howard's argument is that Labour's national and constituency activity failed to sustain much active support. The Labour leadership recognized this to be partly true, acknowledging that Labour failed to win the rural areas, that its national and local newspapers were always in a precarious financial position, and even the urban and industrial strongholds lacked faith when the Labour governments were unable to deliver the improved society they offered. Even in Aberavon, MacDonald's own constituency between 1922 and 1929, it was noted in 1926 that

> with unemployment rising and short-time working now widespread, rank-and-file criticism of the leadership was growing. The future was no longer assured, and at the next election 'JRM will have to work very hard otherwise the seat is lost'.[9]

Howard adds that

> MacDonald was no doubt relieved to leave all this behind and move to the safer and cheaper seat of Seaham Harbour in 1928. MacDonald may well have said that Aberavon finally asked too much of him, but it might be as well to ask whether the leadership expected too much of the local parties. Despite the heady success of the immediate post-war period . . . and the nostalgic testimony of many who battled through the period, the picture gained from local party records does not suggest that this was the golden age of working-class politics.

Many others are not so certain.[10] They feel that the Labour Party was making a determined effort to improve both its national and local organization and that, by and large, they succeeded in doing so. Indeed, the evidence tends to suggest that the Labour Party was well organized and effective in tapping the working-class vote from the First World War and up to the 1930s.

THE 1918 GENERAL ELECTION AND LABOUR PARTY ORGANIZATION

The 1918 general election was the first at which the extended franchise and the new constituency arrangement came into use. Since the franchise had been extended to all males above twenty-one years of age and to all females above thirty, the Labour Party expected to perform better than it had done in the pre-war general elections. *The Times*, in the light of the Labour Party's improving organization between 1916 and 1918, noted that 'it really seems as if the Labour party were better prepared for the election than any other'[11] and that 'Labour in the early days of the contest threw much more vigour into the campaign than the candidates and workers of any other party'.[12] It therefore came as something of a shock when this much strengthened, and potentially more strongly supported party failed to achieve its target of winning 100 seats. Instead it won 57 seats, 61 with additions on the opening of Parliament. What is more, most of the Labour leaders lost their seats. This meant that in effect the Parliamentary Labour Party was, overwhelmingly, dominated by trade unions who sponsored all but eight of the Labour MPs.

The result was most unsatisfactory for the Labour Party, though explicable in terms of the 'coupon' nature of the general election and the political arrangements made between some Liberals and the Conservatives. Such an alliance could not last and the Labour Party was determined to improve its organization and propaganda machine and soon improved its own position as a result.

The Labour Party made rapid advances between the end of the First World War and the 1922 general election. This began from the centre where the National Executive Committee reorganized its activities, by appointing four standing sub-committees – organization and elections, policy and programme, literature, research and finance, and general purposes. Egerton Wake became the Labour Party's national agent and vigorously pursued the policy of giving direction to the rest of the movement, through the organizing of regional and local conferences. By 1922 the Party's nine regions had arranged at least three conferences each, many of which were addressed by Wake, Arthur Henderson the secretary, and a 'star' speaker. Advisory Committees, set up by the National Executive Committee on 13 March 1918 in order to help to develop the Party's policies on a wide range of issues, began to publish reports and statements which added to the body of Labour policies. The Party also acquired a paper, the *Daily Herald*, whose frequent financial crises had forced it to become dependent upon the Party for its existence in 1922. Also, in the wake of the 1918 Franchise Act, the Party formed a women's section under Dr Marion Phillips and appointed regional organizers to attract the newly enfranchised women.

There were deficiencies in the new organization. The Party always lacked adequate national finance, the *Daily Herald*'s circulation difficulties were a constant draw upon its limited financial resources, the Advisory Committees had to be modified and, despite the efforts of Wake, there were never enough full-time agents – a mere 133 in 1922, falling to 111 in 1923. Nevertheless, the Labour Party was benefiting from the support it was gaining from the working class. Even the most rudimentary examination of the minutes of the National Executive Committee suggests the feverish activity that was occurring in the immediate postwar years and, in these early days, it was to be expected that mistakes would be made and that new directions would be sought. Indeed, Labour's performance in the 1922 general election, although much improved on the 1918 general election, drew comment in a Labour Party circular in June 1923, to the effect that:

The results of the [1922] General Election have brought forcibly before us the primary importance both of securing the votes of women electors and of getting a large number of women to take part in an electoral campaign. My Executive Committee is of the opinion that it is essential both for winning and retaining Parliamentary seats that special attention should be given to the whole subject. . . .

The notable results of our methods in organizing women has startled the other parties, who will certainly use their best endeavours to counteract our work. Continual efforts between the times of elections will attempt to make their attempts futile.[13]

There was certainly no complacency among Labour's national leaders; quite the contrary.

The enthusiasm engendered by the Labour Party appears to have lapped over into the local constituencies. However, by the end of the First World War the Labour Party organization in West Yorkshire was little advanced on the chaotic structure of overlapping and competing interests which had existed since the formation of the Labour Representation Committee in 1900. Constituency associations were still evolving against a backcloth of rival political groups, all intent on defending their own interests. Yet the detritus of pre-war Labour politics was quickly absorbed as a more unified Labour Party emerged in 1918 with the reorganization of the constituencies, the extension of the franchise and the introduction of a new Labour constitution. The new party structures that emerged were never perfect; Labour agents complained, as readily as did their Liberal and Conservative counterparts, of the shortage of funds and the dependence of the Party on a small number of activists. Yet more full-time agents were appointed, funds were increased, and organizational and propaganda work was undertaken.

Throughout 1918 Labour constituency parties were formed for all four of the Bradford seats and the Bradford Labour Party formally came into existence on 5 April 1919 – uniting the ILP, the Trades Council and the Workers' Municipal Federation into one Labour group. By 1919, the Bradford Labour movement had a central party organization, four constituency parties and twenty-one ward parties.

This pattern of improved organizational activity was repeated throughout West Yorkshire. The rather amorphous Huddersfield Labour movement was transformed into the more clearly defined Huddersfield Divisional Labour Party in the spring and summer of 1918, following meetings between the Trades Council, the ILP and other interested groups.[14] The Colne Valley Divisional Party was formed in June 1917 and the Leeds City Labour Party reorganized itself in April and May 1918, and promoted the formation of constituency parties in the six divisions which made up Leeds.[15]

Once reorganization was successfully accomplished the main priority of the local parties was to appoint full-time agents. Such an action was not to be taken lightly, for despite the financial contribution from Head Office, it could impose a crippling financial burden upon even well-funded constituencies. Not surprisingly it was the bodies in large towns, such as Bradford, Leeds and Huddersfield, which appointed full-time agents. Most, such as Batley and Morley Divisional Labour Party, relied upon part-time agents whose service they paid for during parliamentary contests.[16] Nevertheless, between 1919 and 1922, the NEC of the Labour Party approved the appointment of five full-time agents in West Yorkshire: T. Ashworth (City of Bradford), D.B. Foster (Leeds South), J. Lawson (Elland), W. Whiteley (Huddersfield) and T. Myers (Spen Valley).[17]

The prime function of the improved Labour system was to secure votes. In a period when the life-expectancy of the *Daily Herald* was uncertain and its editorial stance questionable, it was essential for the local Labour parties to have their own newspapers. The West Yorkshire areas were fortunate in having three established provincial papers, the *Bradford Pioneer*, the *Leeds Weekly Citizen* and the Huddersfield *Citizen* by the end of the First World War. The *Worker* expired in 1920 but the *Huddersfield Citizen* replaced it in 1926 and survived up to the 1960s. In addition, there was the *Yorkshire Factory Times*, started in 1889, which acted as the organ of the Yorkshire textile workers until it ceased publication in April 1926. These weekly publications were also supplemented by a whole flotilla of occasional broadsheets, trade-union quarterlies and Labour journals.

In its day the most prestigious of these newspapers was the *Bradford Pioneer*. Among its illustrious editors was Joseph Burgess, the journalist whose call had led to the formation of the national Independent Labour Party at Bradford in 1893, Willie Leach, Fred Jowett, the first Labour MP for Bradford, and Frank Betts, the father of Barbara Castle. Victor Grayson Feather, later General Secretary of the TUC, was one of its correspondents and its cartoonist, until he left Bradford in 1926, and wrote alongside Margaret McMillan, Ramsay MacDonald and Philip Snowden.

The *Bradford Pioneer* epitomized the propaganda role of these newspapers when it advised its readers:

Don't destroy this paper. Become a Pioneer Pusher. Become a Pioneer. Persuade your friends and workmates to order it. If YOU can sell a few in your workshop let us know and we will send them along. New readers means the extension of Labour's influence in world politics. 'Nuff said'. Get busy.[18]

The Labour Party did 'get busy'. The main focus of its activities was the winning of members and most Labour agencies oscillated between stressing the need to organize women's sections and the broader objective of attracting individual members.

THE WOMEN'S SECTION

The development of the Labour Party was greatly improved by the successful creation of its women's section, although this did bring its own very specific problems. Like all political parties, Labour had to address women's issues once the 1918 Franchise Act had given the vote to all women over the age of thirty, and especially once the age limit was reduced to twenty-one in 1928. It took its first step when the Women's Labour League, formed in 1906, fused with the Labour Party in 1918, to form the basis of the women's section of the Labour Party. In the same year women were offered two seats on the National Executive Committee of the TUC. By 1922 more than 100,000 women had joined the 650 women's sections of local Labour parties. There were also about 35,000 women in the Women's Cooperative Guild which acted with the Labour Party although it was an independent body.[19]

The new women's section divided the country into districts, appointed officials and organized conferences. The North-East District reflected its activities. One report to the National Executive Committee indicated that 'Attention was given to Lancashire and Cheshire, the West Riding of Yorkshire, and the Black Country. . . . Advisory Councils are now in the process of formation in the West Riding of Yorkshire and the Black Country.'[20] Mrs Anderson Fenn was appointed to organize the North-East area and was involved in co-ordinating the Advisory Council of Labour Women for the West Riding of Yorkshire at Leeds in 1919, which subsequently acted as the focus for various women's organizations. Indeed, by 1922 many constituencies had developed a viable women's section and active women's branches.

These improvements raised serious gender issues since the presence of these women's societies began to challenge the Labour Party's degree of commitment to the 'equality of the sexes', for women now helped to define the political agenda. Dr Marion Phillips, of the Women's Labour League, who became the Chief Women's Officer within the Labour Party, emphasized the need for the women's section to integrate with Labour Party politics whereas Margaret Llewellyn Davies, of the Women's Cooperative Guild, suggested that the Labour Party was offering women very little. As a consequence the Labour Party was faced with some division and debate over the need for specific policies for women in the 1920s.

The most obvious points of conflict were to be associated with the female demands for both birth control and family allowances. On the issue of birth control, there were many women within the Labour Party who saw it as the way to release themselves from a cycle of poverty and from constant ill health. The issue emerged strongly in May 1924 when a women's deputation went to John Wheatley, Minister of Health in the first Labour government, asking him to lift the ban that made it illegal for local health authorities to distribute birth control information.[21] Marion Phillips, however, felt that birth control should not become a political issue to divide Labour and there was the fear that the Catholic members within the Labour Party would be upset by the dissemination of information on birth control.[22] The NEC of the Labour Party agreed with this view, and it reported at the Labour Party's Liverpool Conference, 1925

> that the subject of birth control is in its nature not one which should be made a political Party issue, but should remain another upon which members of the Party should be free to hold and promote their individual convictions.[23]

Similar debates developed in connection with the demand for family allowances, which many trade-union leaders, such as Ernest Bevin, objected to. Marion Phillips felt that such a provision would 'increase the irresponsibility of fatherhood' in opposition to the supportive fulsome report of the Women's Cooperative Guild.[24]

Nevertheless, throughout the 1920s there was little evidence that the Labour Party had taken the women's issues on board in the gradualist socialist programmes it offered. There was even less evidence of such commitments in the 1930s. With the collapse of the second Labour government the main purpose of the Party came to be the maintenance of unity in order to recover political power and gender issues became less important. In the final analysis the Labour Party found itself incapable of fully integrating gender issues within its social democratic structure once planning, the survival of the Party, and the rejection of communist attempts to affiliate with the Party became more important than women's issues. Nevertheless, the women's section became an important section of the Party and its organizational growth gave the Labour Party resilience.

INDIVIDUAL MEMBERS AND THE TRADE-UNION MOVEMENT

The impact of Labour's improved organization is to be seen in the growth of the individual membership which the Labour Party's 1918 Constitution permitted. The Huddersfield Labour Party had 500 to 600 members in the late 1920s, the six Leeds constituency parties had between 1,500 and 2,000 members for most of the 1920s and the indications are that the Bradford Labour Party had far in excess of the Leeds figure.[25] Yet, despite such developments, it was the ubiquitous trade-union movement which provided ten or more members to every local Labour Party individual member.

By 1918 the Labour Party was shaped, even if it was not totally dominated, by the trade unions. In 1900 the Labour Representation Committee Executive included seven trade unionists and five socialists. In 1902 it had nine trade unionists, one representative of the trades councils and three socialists (two ILP and one Fabian). The Labour Party Constitution of 1918 allowed for the election of thirteen of the twenty-three members of the new National Executive Committee and allowed trade unions to vote in the election of the rest. Throughout the 1920s, and particularly after 1926, the Joint Council of Labour, which brought together the Parliamentary Labour Party (PLP), the TUC and the Labour Party, became increasingly important in making decisions for the 'constitutional' Labour movement. In 1934 it was renamed the National Council of Labour and the TUC was the most important force on this body, with the presence of Ernest Bevin (from 1932) and Walter Citrine.

If the Labour Party had become the party of the working class it had done so through the agency of the trade-union movement and the price it had to pay was the restriction of its policies to a pale version of Clause Four, introduced gradually and selectively. Using the large block vote of the Transport and General Workers, and other unions, Ernest Bevin was able to dominate Labour Party annual conferences throughout the 1930s on issues such as the threat of fascism. Indeed, Bevin remarked that the Labour Party 'grew out of the bowels of the TUC'.[26] This is not to say that the Labour Party did not have the opportunity to do something to extend its socialist planning, for this often operated in a different sphere from trade unionism, although Bevin and the TUC Economic Planning Committee (1932) were part of the process.[27]

The relationship between the Labour Party and the trade unions was complex and not without major difficulties. It has been suggested that while the Labour Party and the trade unions are often seen as working closely together they frequently developed distinct policies and strategies, which sometimes led to a contentious relationship. Indeed, the metaphor that the Labour Party was the 'offspring of the TUC' is misleading because there has often been a disparity in the policies adopted by both organizations.[28] Nevertheless, the two bodies built up a common set of attitudes and rules between 1900 and 1948 based upon loyalty and anti-communism. For the interwar years, though, there were difficulties as the ground rules were being built up and it is not surprising that there should be some sharp disagreements in their relationships. The Labour Party's 1918 Constitution provided the potential for conflict between the broad socialist goals and the narrower base of trade-union objectives. The use of the Emergency Powers Act by the 1924 Labour government to deal with industrial disputes also created tensions with the trade unions. The reluctance of the Labour government of 1929–31 to abolish the Trades Dispute and Trade Union Act of 1927, which made sympathetic strike action illegal and restricted the flow of trade-union funds to the Labour Party, provided yet another source of conflict. The fact is that the Labour government was dependent upon Liberal Party support to continue in office and the Liberals were opposed to the withdrawal of the 1927 Act. The deflationary policies of the Labour governments of 1924 and 1929–31, their failure to tackle the issue of unemployment and willingness to reduce unemployment benefits in 1931 also added to the strains of this relationship.

The different spheres of influence and responsibilities between the Labour Party and the trade unions have been recognized by many contemporaries. W.J. Brown, of the Civil Service Clerical Association, reflecting upon the 1924 Labour government, expressed the view that there was a general assumption that the Labour Cabinet would apply the policy of the TUC in industrial matters but that the reality was that

> there would be a permanent difference in point of view between Government on the one hand and the Trade Union on the other: and that difference in point of view did not arise from any wickedness on the part of the political side, or on the part of the industrial side, but arose from the fact that the Trade Unions had different functions to follow than the functions of Government.[29]

Walter Citrine, General Secretary of the TUC, wrote that the trade unions did not dominate the Labour Party and suggested that the Labour Party and the trade unions 'work together and consult from time to time when any matter of policy is in question'.[30] Trade-union leaders did not seem to expect too much of the Labour Party in government and in June 1931 the Transport and General Workers' Union admitted that 'the results of the work of Government can rarely be seen in its own lifetime'.[31]

The closeness of the trade unions and the Labour Party clearly challenges the view that Labour was badly organized, as do other factors. Most obviously the tendency of Liberal and Conservative parties to form 'Anti-Socialist' or 'Citizens' alliances at local elections is a reflection of the fact that Labour was making a serious challenge to these parties at the local level.[32] By 1923, the message was clear: Labour was the party of the working class. It had built upon its pre-war and wartime roots and was not the fragile party that Howard suggests.

THE 1923 GENERAL ELECTION AND THE FIRST LABOUR GOVERNMENT, 1924

On 6 December 1923 the Labour Party returned 191 MPs to Parliament, an electoral achievement which permitted it to form the first, minority, Labour government on 22 January 1924. Labour had clearly emerged as the second party of British politics, but its government only survived because the Liberal Party felt that it was too risky, in its own interests, to bring it down. Indeed, the Liberal Party saved it by voting against a motion to reduce the Minister of Labour's salary in May 1924. Nevertheless, MacDonald was not prepared to come to terms with the Liberal Party. He informed a packed House of Commons in his first speech as Prime Minister, in February 1924, that 'Coalitions are detestable, are dishonest'. Although his government was in a minority, it would 'bring before this House proposals to deal with great national and international problems, and we are not afraid of what fate we may meet in the process'.[33]

The first Labour administration achieved very little, other than the introduction of John Wheatley's Housing Act which encouraged local authorities to build houses for renting to the working classes. Indeed, it alienated both trade unionists, over the use of the Emergency Powers Act against strikes, and advanced socialists with regard to the moderation of the rest of its policies. Its attempt to reveal itself as a responsible government, its dependence upon Liberals, and its gradual approach meant that it was almost unable to further socialism either inside or outside Britain. MacDonald's administration had nine members who were or had been associated with the Union of Democratic Control (UDC) but it did nothing to change the Treaty of Versailles, which the UDC saw as the cause of political instability in Europe, and supported the Dawes Plan, an American scheme for helping the Germans to pay their postwar reparations. Its only significant international achievements were that it established diplomatic relations with Soviet Russia and offered the prospect of trade with Russia as a part solution to unemployment in Britain.

The first Labour government lasted almost ten months before being ousted in the furore over the Campbell case, when J.R. Campbell, assistant editor of the *Workers' Weekly*, was arrested and charged with incitement to mutiny by the Attorney General and then released because he was only assistant editor of the paper. The resulting debate and vote of no confidence in the House of Commons led to MacDonald's resignation and an election which saw the publication of the infamous, and potentially damaging, Zinoviev Letter, which suggested that the Communist Party was using the Labour Party to achieve its own revolutionary objectives.

Out of office for four and a half years, the Labour Party drifted under MacDonald's leadership. There were certainly tensions between the leading figures and various suggestions that J.R. Clynes, the Vice-Chairman of the Parliamentary Labour Party, or Philip Snowden should take over. There was also some frustration at MacDonald's comparatively limited action during the General Strike of 1926, although the Chairman and the Chief Whip of the Parliamentary Labour Party were invited to all the TUC's General Council meetings with the Miners' Executive in order to co-ordinate industrial and parliamentary activity.[34] This increasing frustration with MacDonald was exhibited in a letter from Snowden attached to the MacDonald diaries. Having suggested that some tensions between them should be ended he wrote that:

> you must excuse me from writing quite so plainly. I am expressing the feeling of all my colleagues who have talked to me on the subject. We are feeling that somehow – it is difficult to explain – we cannot get inside you. You seem to be protected by some impenetrable barrier. I called it aloofness in my last letter. It was not so in the old days of the NAC [of the ILP].[35]

RAMSAY MACDONALD AND THE SECOND LABOUR GOVERNMENT, MAY 1929 TO AUGUST 1931

The second Labour government, also a minority one, took Labour's commitment to state socialism, or public ownership, no further than the first had done. It came into power in May 1929 at a time when the economy was improving and unemployment falling but was set back by the Wall Street Crash of November 1929 and its disastrous economic impact upon world trade. Faced with rising unemployment, increasing expenditure and financial imbalances, MacDonald's government was forced to accept the all-party Sir George May Committee examination of the national finances in 1931 and the need to introduce massive public expenditure cuts if Britain was to remain on the gold standard and to continue to operate a free-trade economy. It was the Labour government's attempt to balance the budget that raised the prospect of the 10 (initially 20) per cent cut in unemployment benefits, which divided the Labour Cabinet on 23 and 24 August 1931, and paved the way for the formation of MacDonald's National government. The very fact that the Labour Cabinet discussed a cut in unemployment benefit demonstrated that its commitment to a decent standard of living for those who could not be guaranteed work, something the Labour Party had stressed since the 'Right to Work' campaign of 1908, was meaningless. It also demonstrated that the second Labour government and Philip Snowden, its Chancellor of the Exchequer, were slaves to the Treasury dogma of balancing the budget.

The collapse of the second Labour government has, of course, produced immense debate. Since the 1930s it has been usual for Labour sympathizers to argue that MacDonald had betrayed the second Labour government and carried out his 'long-thought-out plan'. L. MacNeill Weir captured the spirit of accusations levelled against MacDonald, maintaining that he was never a socialist, was an opportunist, that he schemed to ditch the Labour government and that he was guilty of betrayal. In 1938, Weir wrote that:

> The members of the Labour Cabinet naturally assumed on that Saturday night, 23 August (1931) that Mr. Baldwin would be asked to form a government. But it is significant that MacDonald had something quite different in view. Without a word of consultation with his Cabinet colleagues, without even informing them of his

intention to set up a National Government with himself as Prime Minister he proceeded to carry out his long-thought-out plan.[36]

This view has been challenged by David Marquand and other writers. Marquand insists that there is little to suggest that MacDonald schemed to ditch the second Labour government and that MacDonald's only fault was that he held on to his nineteenth-century principles too long. MacDonald's almost religious acceptance of the gold standard and free trade, plus his belief in the primacy of the state over party, ensured that he lacked the 'ability and willingness to jettison cherished assumptions in the face of changing realities'.[37]

The available evidence suggests that Marquand is correct. MacDonald was as good a socialist as any of the early Labour leaders, writing for the Socialist Library, and committed to the gradual extension of state powers over industry. He was an opportunist but gave up his chairmanship of the Parliamentary Labour Party in 1914 in order to oppose the First World War. There is no specific evidence to suggest that MacDonald intended to bring about the end of the second Labour government, only innuendo and speculation. Indeed, Malcolm MacDonald, Ramsay's son, records that his father had telephoned him at lunchtime on 22 August to the effect that 'He feels pretty certain that he will resign either tonight or tomorrow', and there is compelling evidence that he was contemplating a political career in Labour's back benches.[38] Partial as this source is it is obvious that, given the economic circumstances, it would have been difficult for MacDonald to have arranged the type of political scheming contemplated by his critics.[39] It was the need to cut expenditure in the drive to balance the budget and secure loans from abroad, in order to keep Britain on a gold standard and free-trade system, that forced the Cabinet to agree, by eleven votes to nine, to reduce unemployment benefits by 10 per cent. It was clear that the Cabinet was fairly evenly divided and this seems to have prompted MacDonald to take the resignations of his Cabinet to King George V. It was only a confluence of other events – including the support of the opposition leaders for a National government headed by MacDonald and the appeal of the King – that led MacDonald to form the National government with the support of the Conservative and Liberal parties and some prominent Labour figures, including Philip Snowden and Jimmy Thomas.

MacDonald's action led to the condemnation of the Labour Party and the trade unions, so that when the financial crisis did occur the issue was not the future of socialism. Instead it became a conflict between the second Labour government, committed to operating the gold standard and free trade and thus faced with reducing government expenditure and unemployment benefits, and a TUC which felt that any such action would be a betrayal of the interests of the working classes. This was evident on 20 August 1931 when a deputation from the General Council of the TUC, along with a deputation from the Labour Party Executive, met with members of the Labour Cabinet, including Snowden and MacDonald. There was certainly no meeting of minds between on the one hand, MacDonald and Snowden, and on the other, Bevin, Citrine, A. Hayday and A. Pugh. Citrine denied that the economic situation was desperate for 'There are enormous resources in this country.'[40] It was clear that neither the Labour Cabinet nor the TUC were going to come to an accommodation and the Labour Cabinet split soon afterwards and paved the way for the formation of a National government. They were even less enamoured of MacDonald when his National government moved off the gold standard in September 1931, an action which had it been taken in August might have reduced the need for some expenditure cuts and allowed the second Labour government to continue.

CONCLUSION

Between 1918 and 1931 the Labour Party had clearly established its political supremacy in British progressive politics, turning its working-class, women's, and trade-union vote into parliamentary success. It had become a party of government but had, at the end of this period, to withstand the defection of Ramsay MacDonald, one of its formative leaders, who left the Party apparently driven on by his sense of national duty rather than some compulsion to abandon and betray Labour. Although this posed a serious challenge to Labour, which it was to overcome, it is clear that the Labour Party had truly become the party of the working class and progressive interests in British politics, and the second party of government.

CHAPTER FOUR

The Collapse and Revival of Labour, c. 1931–45

The years between 1931 and 1945 saw both the Labour Party's collapse as a parliamentary force, as a result of MacDonald's defection, and its rapid recovery to a point whereby it was able to form its first majority government, after its landslide victory in the 1945 general election. Thus, these years saw both the low point and the high point of Labour's political fortunes. The reality is, of course, that Labour's recovery was less dramatic than at first appears, since its parliamentary decline in 1931 was due to unusual political circumstances which saw it opposed by an alliance of the other political parties. Its recovery and success was to be expected and, as a result of the Second World War, it was thrust forward to political power.

LABOUR'S ORGANIZATIONAL AND POLICY DEVELOPMENTS IN THE 1930s

The general election of October 1931 saw the Labour Party reduced to a mere 52 MPs from the 289 in 1929 and the National government secured 556 seats, a majority of 497. Philip Snowden's attack upon Labour's election policy as 'Bolshevism Run Mad' had helped to take a toll on Labour's strength. Why this defeat occurred and what it meant for Labour Party politics has been open to question. It would appear that Labour had lost almost 2 million votes, down from about 8.4 million in 1929 to 6.65 million in 1931. This might well have been the result of the financial events surrounding the collapse of the Labour government impacting upon the election results, although it has been suggested that the result was more to do with the Labour Party frustrating its supporters and performing badly in parliamentary by-elections in 1930 and 1931: 'The simple reason why Labour had lost four out of five seats it was defending was that its opponents were united.'[1] Indeed, there were 449 straight fights against Labour in 1931 compared with only 99 in 1929.

Labour reacted well to this defeat. It realized that its organization remained strong, and its local parties recovered quickly, by November 1932, making good some of the municipal losses they had incurred in November 1931. It also began to revitalize the Party with a 'Million New Members Campaign' in 1932, which had increased individual membership by 100,000 within a year. In January 1933 it set up a Central By-Election Insurance Fund to help needy constituencies put forward candidates. In the leadership stakes, Arthur Henderson gave way to George Lansbury and, in 1935, Clement Attlee, a young and far more effective leader, emerged to lead the Labour Party for the next twenty years. The result of the improved organization of the Party can be seen in the fact that in the 1935 general election Labour won 154 seats and gained a vote of 8,325,491, which was only 64,000 fewer than the number who had voted for Labour at the successful 1929 general election.

DEVELOPMENT OF SOCIALIST POLICY

Yet organizational developments alone do not account for Labour's recovery; it also owed a great deal to the discussion about socialist policies, and particularly public ownership. The state was to be the Labour Party's vehicle for achieving socialism, the redistribution of income and wealth throughout society on a more equitable basis, and the Webbs embroidered this with the idea of a 'Social Parliament' which would administer the major industries and services through many tiers of committees. Those who challenged this commitment to statist socialism were ignored. Moreover, at the 1920 Labour Party Conference resolutions were carried demanding the more effective publicizing of the Labour Party's plans for the nationalization of land, gas, water, electricity and banking and for the creation of workers' committees, district councils and national boards.[2] The 1922 Labour Party Conference had established this policy by a commitment to the nationalization of land, mines and 'other essential public services' in the Party's election programme.[3] The Independent Labour Party had attempted to drive the Labour Party into committing itself to more radical proposals in its 'Socialism in Our Time' campaign of 1926 and 1927, but the Labour Party would not be pushed. Instead, Labour responded with its own programme *Labour and the Nation* (1928) which accepted some of the demands of 'Socialism in Our Time', including public ownership, though not of the Bank of England and the joint stock banks. It adopted a 'step by step' approach and stated that the Labour Party would 'without haste, but without rest, with careful preparation, with the use of the best technical knowledge and managerial skills, and with due compensation to the persons affected' socialize the basic industries. Of the ideology of the Party it spoke of 'tentative doctrineless socialism' brought about 'by experimental methods, without violence or disturbances'.[4] *Labour and the Nation* was accepted by the Party Conference in 1928.[5]

By 1931, then, the Labour Party had identified a number of industries it wished to nationalize, with due compensation and in the fullness of time. Yet the MacDonald defection of 1931 led to the questioning of the 'inevitability of gradualness' and to the realization that Labour lacked a policy on many important domestic issues.

There had to be a more detailed commitment to public ownership and an alternative socialist strategy needed to be developed in the place of the discredited policies of Labour's departed leaders. In fact, Labour's 1931 general election manifesto, *Labour's Call to Action: The Nation's Opportunity*, revealed a modest leftward drift, blamed the crisis on capitalist breakdown and advocated public ownership and planning as the solution to Britain's economic problems.

R.H. Tawney and Stafford Cripps also began to consider the need for a more speedy transition to socialism on the grounds that slow change was unlikely to undermine the capitalist base from which it would emerge and got the 1933 Labour Party Conference to accept a resolution committing a future Labour government to introduce socialism immediately.[6] Yet the dilemma faced was that of reconciling their schemes with the demands of a far more cautious trade-union movement dominated by Bevin, which particularly wanted a programme of practical policies which could easily be applied to reduce the high level of unemployment. Indeed, Bevin had produced his *My Plan for 2,000,000 Workless* in 1932 which advocated a variety of schemes including the reduction of retirement age, the raising of the school leaving age and the creation of work by starting major building schemes. His focus was extremely narrow and social rather than socialism, and one is reminded that there were, in the 1920s, some obvious differences between the trade-union leaders and the Labour Party. The trade unions stressed the democratic right to decide about wages and conditions of employment while the Labour Party claimed and operated a system of parliamentary privilege.[7]

This may explain why the trade-union domination of the Labour Party in the 1930s did not inhibit the social planning that was evident within the intellectual socialist groups. In the end the moderate and right-wing socialists in the Labour Party prevailed and developed their policies under the guise of planning.

Labour's social planning was conducted mainly by the New Fabian Research Bureau (1931), the TUC Economic Committee (1932) and a new policy committee of the National Executive Committee of the Labour Party, with four sub-committees, created for the purpose in 1931. The most important of these NEC sub-committees was that for Finance and Trade chaired by Hugh Dalton, who virtually wrote Labour's economic and financial policy in the 1930s. None the less, few of these policies would have had influence without the support of the National Council of Labour (an amalgam of the executives of the TUC, the PLP and the Labour Party) and thus the support of Bevin and Citrine, who dominated this body, was vital. Therefore, there was never likely to be a commitment to full-scale reorganization of British industry since that would require a complete change in the relations between the state and the economy, which Bevin was not prepared to contemplate in the short term.

A commitment to nationalizing the joint stock banks was agreed at the Labour Party Conference of 1932, and driven by the Labour left.[8] Yet such radicalism was not to last as, over the next few years, Labour restricted itself to a policy of nationalizing the Bank of England and became increasingly attracted to the policies of J.M. Keynes, who suggested that economic policies could achieve full employment through indirect controls.

Dalton was the power behind Labour's new and moderate, but planned, socialist policies. Essentially committed to the gradual extension of state control he dismissed the rival alternatives put forward and argued that 'Labour needed better policies and better people'.[9] At first, he joined Cole's New Fabian Research Bureau as a member of its directing body, visiting the Soviet Union with a group of New Fabians in the summer of 1932. He returned convinced that the First and Second Five Year Plans of the Soviet Union indicated that planning could work and that Britain required something similar, though not under a communist regime. From then onwards, planning socialism in Britain became Dalton's main objective. He wanted to redistribute the resources of Britain in order to tackle the appalling problem of unemployment and he took this commitment into the NEC's eight-man Policy Committee where he emerged as Chairman of the Finance and Trade Sub-

Committee. Here he maintained the belief that planning was to be free from market pressures, have the ability to overcome official resistance and should call upon experts. According to his Labour Party document *Socialism and the Condition of the People* (1933), there ought to be 'a well-planned rush'.[10] When this was debated at the 1933 Labour Party Conference it was accepted that there was a need to nationalize joint stock banks, the steel industry and other vital industries. Nevertheless, there was a mixed economy element in Dalton's proposals.

Dalton's influence was further evident in Labour's new policy document *For Socialism and Peace*, one of the most radical policy documents ever presented by Labour, which was accepted by the Party Conference in 1934 and made specific commitments to planning and nationalization while not specifying which industries would be subject to public ownership. This was a very contentious document which was criticized for being rather general, but it had gained widespread support at the 1934 Conference for it was 'based on a concordat between political moderates and their trade union counterparts'.[11]

The policies outlined in *For Socialism and Peace* were more closely examined by Dalton in his *Practical Socialism for Britain* (1935), which emphasized that planning under capitalism was possible and maintained that it could speed up the transition to socialism. It played down the importance of Keynesian commitment to expanding the economy out of slump but acknowledged the importance of a National Investment Board to control and direct the level of long-term investment. The emphasis was, however, to be placed upon the nationalization of basic industries.[12]

These schemes were played down further during the November 1935 general election but shortly afterwards the TUC presented specific plans for the socialization of the cotton industry to the 1935 Labour Party Conference. They, and other proposals, were eventually distilled into *Labour's Immediate Programme*, adopted at the Party Conference in 1937, which removed the commitment to nationalize joint stock banks but committed Labour to a limited programme of nationalization. Thus, in almost twenty years, the Labour Party had moved from an unspecified commitment to public ownership to offering a modest programme of nationalization and state intervention which was to provide a blueprint for the postwar Attlee governments. It lacked the radicalism that some socialists had hoped for, and there were no new radical ideas. Yet five years of policy discussions had at least committed Labour to a specific, if restricted, set of proposals for public ownership.

This policy commitment and activity was quickly transmitted to the local level. The scale of occupational and propaganda work was enormous. There were vast eruptions of activity in even the weakest of constituency parties. The Bradford Labour Party held a 'Victory for Socialism' conference in 1934, Labour League of Youth organizations began to expand, and parliamentary by-election victories – such as Arthur Greenwood's at Wakefield in April 1932 – provided the impetus for further propaganda work.

Very quickly, the Labour Party also became identified with several immediate issues of the day. It was involved in the attempt to fight against the Household Means Test introduced by the MacDonald National government, now essentially a Conservative administration in which an isolated MacDonald attended to foreign policy while Stanley Baldwin and Neville Chamberlain dominated domestic policy. Labour's representatives occupied positions on the Public Assistance committees (local authority based bodies which had replaced the boards of guardians of the Poor Law in 1930), in the hope of nudging relief provisions upwards, and its councillors were responsible for many public schemes – most notably the tremendous slum-clearance and house-building schemes which occurred in Leeds during the mid-1930s. These activities strengthened the already close links with the trade-union movement.

The unity between the Labour Party and the trade unions, despite the tendency to operate in different spheres, prevented the intrusion of more radical socialist proposals. In particular, it kept at bay some of the alternative revolutionary ideas of the Communist Party of Great Britain.

Labour and the Communist Party of Great Britain: The 1920s Context and Relations in the 1930s

From its formation in 1920 and until 1928, the Communist Party of Great Britain (CPGB) attempted to affiliate with the Labour Party. This caused much consternation within the Labour Party which, while rejecting the CPGB's application at its annual conferences, found it impossible to exclude individual communists from its proceedings. The problem was that the Labour Party was dominated by the trade unions who could, and did, send a small number of communist delegates to the Labour Party conferences and, indeed, to local Labour Party constituency meetings much against the wishes of their national trade-union leaders. Faced with its own version of 'the enemy within', the Labour Party sought to remove the offending delegates and began a long process of finding the right formulation of resolutions which would exclude communists without offending some rank-and-file trade unionists.

Labour's first main attack upon communist infiltration began at the Labour Party's Edinburgh Conference of 1922, when it was agreed that every person nominated to serve as a delegate 'shall individually accept the constitution and principles of the Labour Party'.[13] This decision was supported by a resolution that delegates could not be associated with any party wishing to return MPs who were not approved by the Labour Party.

The Edinburgh amendments directly challenged the right of trade unions to determine who would be their representatives at Labour Party conferences and called upon local parties to exclude properly accredited communist representatives from their ranks. Even though communists were very thin on the ground, local Labour parties began to jib at the prospect of excluding 'tried and trusted' members and delegates from trade-union branches, simply because they were members of the CPGB.

Such was the hostility to the Edinburgh amendments that the London Conference of the Labour Party, held in the summer of 1923, agreed to drop the second amendment and to rely upon the first, which simply asked that all delegates should individually accept the constitution of the Labour Party. In December 1923 the NEC of the Labour Party decided to form a sub-committee to examine the whole issue. It first reported to the full NEC on 2 September 1924 and later that month endorsed the view that the affiliation of the CPGB had to be refused and that no member of that party could be eligible for endorsement as a Labour candidate for Parliament or any public body.[14] The sub-committee emphasized the great variance between the Labour and Communist parties: 'The Labour Party seeks to achieve the Socialist Commonwealth by means of Parliamentary democracy. The Communist Party seeks to achieve the "Dictatorship of the Proletariat" by armed revolution.'[15] It saw no way in which a party which favoured 'tyranny' could be affiliated to the Labour Party. The NEC endorsed this decision in December 1924 and reminded local Labour parties that it would be a breach of the Labour Party Constitution for them to ignore the decision to exclude communists. The debate continued throughout 1925 and 1926 until the Party Conference of 1926 reiterated the decisions first taken at Edinburgh in 1922.

This policy remained the basis of the Labour Party's attitude towards the CPGB thereafter. Throughout the rest of the interwar years, however, the attitude of the CPGB towards Labour changed on two counts. Firstly, the General Strike of 1926 led to a conflict between the CPGB and the TUC, in which the trade-union leaders tried to isolate and reduce communist support within the trade-union movement. Secondly, in 1928 the Comintern, the Third International, decided to withdraw from its 'United Front' policy and attack the Labour Party in its 'Class Against Class' policy, accusing the Labour Party of being the third capitalist party in Britain, although it would appear that the CPGB was already moving in that direction from 1926.[16] The CPGB now declared its revolutionary programme, in which Great Britain would become a Workers' Socialist Republic with a programme of nationalization, workers' state farms, shorter hours of work and better working conditions.[17] In one fell swoop 'Class Against Class' killed off communist support within the Labour Party and put Communist Party candidates against Labour candidates at the 1929 general election.[18]

The CPGB attempted to revive its links with the Labour Party in the 1930s but with little success, although, as will be suggested later, it gained some modest success in winning trade-union support.[19] In 1933 the threat of European fascism led to the CPGB re-instituting the United Front (of socialist parties), in this case against fascism. By 1935 the CPGB was even attempting to operate a Popular Front, willing to work with all anti-fascist parties. Once again, the CPGB was attempting to affiliate to the Labour Party but without any success, despite the fact that there were often hundreds of declarations of support for such a policy at the Labour Party Conferences.

Hitler's accession to the chancellorship of Germany in January 1933 and the Spanish Civil War between 1936 and 1939, brought into the open the Labour Party's continued antipathy towards the CPGB. The Labour left were particularly interested in the communist-inspired United and Popular Front campaigns against fascism. The United Front's purpose was to forge an alliance between socialist and communist organizations while the Popular Front, of the late 1930s, was more an ethical alliance of progressive interests against the failures of British foreign policy aimed at an alliance with all anti-fascist organizations. Be that as it may, the fact is that the Labour Party saw the United Front and the Popular Front as part of the communist challenge to its position, and was unwilling to be involved.

This became more obvious in the case of the Spanish Civil War, where General Franco was leading a forced rebellion against the Spanish Republican government. The United Front and Popular Front evoked little support from the Labour Party leadership and the TUC. Labour leaders participated in the general humanitarian concern for Spain but did not wish to unite with the CPGB in campaigning for a more active involvement in Spanish affairs. Indeed, as will be seen later, because of its support of the Popular Front against fascism the Socialist League, a body of left-wing socialists in the Labour Party dedicated to uniting socialist organizations against fascism, was forced to disband in 1937.

Yet it is not at all clear that the Labour Party/TUC opposition to the Popular Front in connection with Spain was entirely about hostility to the CPGB. In fact, it has been noted of the Spanish Civil War, that 'The Labour Party did not see it as the "last Great Cause" but as a problem to be overcome', and that 'the Catholic minority [within trade unions] acted as a storm-centre for opposition to the Spanish Republic'.[20] For instance, Ernest Bevin's sympathies were with the Republicans but he refused to be influenced by the emotions generated by Spain because of the problems within his own union, the Transport and General Workers' Union (TGWU). At the time the TGWU had a strong core of Catholic supporters among the Liverpool dockers, who were being encouraged by Catholic priests to criticize Republican actions, including the murdering of priests, in Spain. This section objected to the TGWU for sending about £1,000 of humanitarian aid to Spain. At the same time, and among many of the so-called rank-and-file communist members of the TGWU in London, there were equally vociferous demands to give more trade-union support for the removal of the National government's embargo against arms being sent to Spain, which was particularly damaging the position of the legitimate Spanish Republican government.[21] Ernest Bevin and the TGWU were thus criticized, at one and the same time, for both doing too much for the Spanish Republican government and for doing too little.[22] Other trade unions, and the Labour Party, faced a similar dilemma.

Therefore, it could be argued that the Labour Party was not prepared to put its full weight of support behind the Spanish Republican government. This may have had something to do with the fact that it was a government run by communists but it should be remembered that Spain did pose a problem for both the Labour Party and the trade unions and that support for the Republican side was more muted and circumscribed than it might otherwise have been, even allowing for the symbolic visits to Spain by Labour leaders such as Clement Attlee. As far as the Labour Party was concerned the presence of what were perceived to be communist-inspired United and Popular Fronts did not help matters. The Labour Party was not prepared to accept communists at the national level and this was an attitude that they sought to pass on to constituency Labour parties by the late 1930s.[23]

Nevertheless, from the middle to the end of the 1930s communists were present within the local trade-union movements and hence the local Labour Party constituency organizations. The Socialist League, a body of about 3,000 members, was one society which encouraged this development for it associated itself with the Popular Front demands in the 1930s.[24] Indeed, there was significant support for the United Front and the Popular Front from the Labour left and it has been observed that 'the dividing line between the Communist Party and the Labour left was virtually indefinable, not least because an unknown number of communists pursued their Popular Front activities within the Labour Party'.[25] Yet the Labour Party had shut the door on the CPGB and, by the end of the 1930s, had developed a fairly extensive system of proscription, excluding individuals and organizations who supported the CPGB or its official line. In fact, the Socialist League was forced to disband in May 1937 and Cripps, Aneurin Bevan, and those who supported what were referred to as 'Crippisms', were expelled from the Labour Party in a flurry of activity in January 1939.[26]

Local Labour parties began to take action and watched their dissentients more carefully. The Leeds Labour Party, for instance, was particularly concerned about the Leeds branch of the Militant Labour League. Formed about 1938 by Lancelot Lake, the Leeds branch of the League attacked the local Leeds Labour Party, focused upon the need to face up to both fascism and capitalism, campaigned for the setting up of an International Workers' Socialist Republic and called upon 'Socialists not to leave the Labour Party . . . but to join with us in building the Organised Socialist Left Wing'.[27] The Leeds Labour Party kept a file on this branch and had A.L. Williams, Secretary of the Leeds Labour Party and editor of its newspaper the *Leeds Citizen*, keep a check on this organization and other suspected communist individuals and groups. The relationship between the Labour left and the communists was clearly an issue of great importance to the Labour Party.

FASCISM AT HOME AND ABROAD

The Labour Party's hostility towards communism had clearly raised the issue of its attitude towards both British and foreign fascist movements.

Unwilling to join with the CPGB as a 'United Front against Fascism', the Labour Party played down the importance of fascism at home, though not abroad.

There were few centres of fascist support in Britain, outside London, Manchester, Birmingham and Leeds. The Labour Party's 1934 circular on fascism revealed the thinness of support. Even in Leeds, one of the best organized of fascist centres, it found only 100 to 200 fascists. Indeed, when Mosley addressed a meeting of 1,500 people at Leeds Town Hall in May 1934 it was estimated that about 400 fascists were present, 'most of whom had come by bus'.[28]

Drawing from this evidence, it was suggested that there was no point in planning Labour action against the British Union of Fascists (BUF). The Olympia BUF meeting of 7 June 1934, in which fascists clashed with communists, seemed unnecessary to the Labour Party, especially since right-wing Conservative support for the BUF also began to disappear at the same time. Labour's attitude remained that it was pointless to fight fascism on the streets of Britain since it would draw attention to an insignificant organization. While the Labour Party was, probably, quite right to play down the fascist challenge it could not ignore the threat of European fascism.

Throughout the interwar years Labour politicians had been concerned about the need to preserve peace. They posed numerous questions. Could European peace be guaranteed by disarmament? Could French fears of, and hostility towards, Germany be removed? To these and similar questions they offered three policies for peace in Europe: disarmament, collective security through the League of Nations, and the restoration to Germany of her territories removed by the Treaty of Versailles. It was widely believed that these policies would provide the basis of peaceful co-existence between nations. Yet mutual distrust between France and Germany persisted, Hitler rose to power in Germany, the Spanish Civil War presented the stark challenge of fascism, and the Italian intervention in Abyssinia revealed the contempt which the Italians had for the League of Nations. Some Labour politicians continued to cling to their previous peace strategies but by the end of the 1930s the majority had come to accept that the Second World War was inevitable – a view confirmed by the events in Czechoslovakia, Austria and Poland which preceded the outbreak of the European war. This change of attitude created problems for the large and cumbersome structure of the Labour Party, where the commitment to peace was a deep and sensitive issue. In a slow, confused process of adjustment the Labour

Party attuned itself to the fight against fascism, and eventually the need to abandon its emphasis upon political isolation.

It was Ernest Bevin and the trade-union movement which forced the Labour Party to change direction. In 1933, at the Hastings Conference, the Party had shown its commitment to two potentially contradictory policies. It supported a resolution committing it to organize working-class action, including a general strike, to oppose war but also supporting one accepting the need for a general reduction of armaments within the security of the League of Nations' commitment to take action against aggressor states. The difficulty was that Labour could have found itself supporting military action against a fascist state at the same time as it threatened a general strike against war.

In fact the Labour Party was divided on how to maintain peace. Arthur Henderson, Ernest Bevin, Hugh Dalton and Clement Attlee, and their supporters, favoured disarmament based upon the collective security of the League of Nations. The young Hugh Gaitskell, who had become aware of the dangers of fascism on his visit to Austria in the summer of 1933, later summed up the problem of this approach by arguing that a general strike against all wars was an 'invitation to the fascist aggressors'.[29] A second, rather smaller, group led by George Lansbury, the Party leader, advocated pacifism. A third, composed of ex-members of the Independent Labour Party, favoured an international general strike to prevent the conflict and the need for working-class institutions to offer a revolutionary programme. A fourth, led by Sir Stafford Cripps and the Socialist League, a body founded in 1932 mainly from members of the Independent Labour Party who did not wish to leave the Labour Party, favoured a 'United Front' with the communists against the fascists. Cripps explained that the fascist threat was serious and that the Communist Party hostility towards the Labour Party had now changed and was more favourable.

These factions came into conflict at the 1935 Labour Party Conference. This took place at Brighton in the climate of Italian aggression against Abyssinia, and Ernest Bevin, with the overwhelming support of the trade-union movement, swept away the protests of Lansbury and Cripps's Socialist League to win conference support for the collective security, through the League of Nations' sanctions, against Italian aggression in Abyssinia. Bevin, with the support of the trade unions, put paid to any pacifist policies which George Lansbury still harboured for the Labour Party. Bevin dealt brutally with Lansbury and his pacifist reservations, thus forcing him to quit as leader of the Labour Party. Rather dramatically Hugh Dalton recorded that Bevin 'hammered [Lansbury] to death'.[30]

This Conference also provoked two major and related controversies: the Socialist League mounted a major challenge against the Conference policy and constituency parties began to protest that the block-vote of trade unions was limiting their influence within the Party. The Socialist League and the constituencies were linked by the common membership of Sir Stafford Cripps. Defeated at the 1935 Labour Party Conference, the Socialist League and Cripps attempted to forge alliances with other socialist groups to promote the 'United Front against Fascism'. Cripps's link with the constituency parties' movement gave the Socialist League more influence in promoting its demands.

The Abyssinian crisis and the Spanish Civil War tended to confirm the conflicting views of both extremes of the Labour Party. At one extreme, Bevin and Dalton, who were opposed to Labour associating in any way with the Communist Party of Great Britain, felt that the invasion of Spain by Franco's fascist forces justified rearmament. Peace was to be maintained by rearmament, even if one had to rely upon the National government to take action and work through the League of Nations. At the other extreme, Cripps and the Socialist League supported the 'United Front' campaign of socialist organizations, initially put forward by the Communist Party, because they felt that the National government was unlikely to face up to the fascist threat in Europe, and that rearmament was not safe in its hands. As a result, the Edinburgh Labour Party Conference of 1936 passed contradictory resolutions leaving the Party supporting collective international rearmament but opposing national rearmament, thus meeting the requirements of the two conflicting sets of opinion within the Labour Party. However, the Spanish Civil War did make a difference. The conference condemned the non-intervention policy adopted by the major powers, for it was being flouted by Italians, Germans and Russians, and recommended that the Spanish Republican government should be allowed to buy arms.[31]

After the Conference, the Socialist League continued to oppose rearmament, opposed sanctions threatened against Italy as a result of the Italian invasion of Abyssinia, and advocated for the Labour movement a policy of preparing for the 'mass resistance to war'; by which it meant a general strike. In January 1937 it patched together a new 'United Front' campaign in association with the Independent Labour Party, the Communist Party of Great Britain, the Left Book Club and *Tribune* (a left-wing journal), around a programme of defence for the Spanish Republic, opposition to the National government, support for the struggles of the unemployed and the affiliation of the CPGB and the ILP to the Labour Party. The campaign was in defiance of the Labour Party ban on joint work with the CPGB and the Socialist League was condemned by the Labour Party, its members being forced to choose between disbanding the organization or expulsion from the Labour Party. The Socialist League was thus dissolved in May 1937.

The Communist Party of Great Britain had mounted its 'Popular Front against Fascism' at the Seventh Congress of the Comintern (Communist International) in July/August 1935. This broad front, of all those opposed to fascism, had been partly taken up by Cripps but was extended in 1937 and 1938. Yet Cripps's campaign, supported by Aneurin Bevan, was rejected by the Labour Party, which expelled both of them in 1939.

Nevertheless, by 1939 the Labour Party was prepared to fight fascism. Indeed, they had already strongly opposed both fascism and appeasement at their 1937 Bournemouth Conference, calling for the National government to abandon its non-intervention policy in Spain. When war broke out in Europe in September 1939 the Party was, therefore, willing to support the National government against German aggression.

THE LABOUR PARTY 1939–45

The Labour Party firmly supported Neville Chamberlain's declaration of war on Germany on 3 September 1939, and agreed to an 'Electoral Truce', though it initially refused to join the Chamberlain government in the prosecution of the war. However, it did not enter the Coalition government until May 1940, when Winston Churchill replaced Neville Chamberlain as Prime Minister. Labour did well out of the allocation of offices in the new government and benefited politically at the end of the war. But was Labour's revival and success in the 1945 general election primarily a result of the wartime experience?

There is certainly much evidence that Labour was reviving in the 1930s, after the political fiasco of 1931. In addition, it is possible that there was a new popular radicalism emerging in Britain.[32] The bombing and evacuation at the beginning of the war had exposed social problems which had hitherto remained hidden from public view and generated a sense of commitment by central government to the strategic necessity of having a contented and healthy civilian population. However, some writers on the Second World War have been far more cautious and ambivalent. It has been argued that the war helped to establish a new political consensus and that the leftward shift in popular attitudes began as early as 1940 with the appointment of sixteen Labour ministers to Churchill's wartime government, the emphasis that was placed upon establishing a fairer society and the organization of wartime evacuations. Yet the crucial factor in the change appears to have been the military catastrophe at Dunkirk, which seems to have forced the wartime government, faced with the need to restore calm and instil unity into the war effort, to offer welfare provisions for all. In the wake of Dunkirk, William Beveridge, and many of the Whitehall mandarins, began to organize the war effort and, according to one writer, 'The home front organised for war was becoming a model, and an inspiration, for the reorganisation of the peace.'[33] Nevertheless, the atmosphere of optimistic solidarity was by no means as universal as some have supposed. Yet Labour benefited from those social changes for the new consensus represented a 'dilution of Conservative rather than Labour politics'.[34] Indeed, it appears that the mood of the nation was changing rapidly between 1940 and 1942 and that the Labour Party profited from the barrage of wartime activity and propaganda.

Such an assessment has been broadly supported by a wide range of historians.[35] Whatever their individual views on the nature of the impact of war, they are clear that the Labour Party was the great beneficiary of the growth of wartime radicalism. Even those who have criticized the whole episode whereby wartime radicalism imposed upon Britain a commitment to a postwar welfare state, admit to the impetus this gave to the political popularity of the Labour Party.[36]

There seems little doubt that the Labour Party benefited more than other parties from the wartime radicalism, although there has been some questioning of the extent to which there was wartime consensus.[37] The only significant difference of opinion seems to be the timing of this changed political mood. There was a leftward swing in political opinion in the early 1940s. Certainly, by 1942 there was evidence of rising political support for Labour in the opinion polls run by Gallup, and in December 1942, Mass Observation estimated that about two people out of five had changed their political outlook since the beginning of the Second World War.[38] The new wartime radicalism may not have been a 'formed socialist ideology', but it was an outlook that the Labour Party could put to good use.[39]

The Labour Party was well prepared to deal with the war, unlike in 1914. From the beginning it was looking to the future, in a way which the Conservative Party (whose wartime organization seemed to be waning quickly) did not. Stealing a march on the other political parties, Labour produced *Labour War Aims* in October 1939 and *Labour, the War and Peace* and *Labour's Home Policy* in 1940. In these statements, the Labour Party outlined the way in which a strengthened League of Nations could be used to maintain the peace 'once the rule of law' had brought about peace. But of more immediate importance was Labour's belief that 'for the Labour Party a Socialist Britain is not some far-out Utopia, but an ideal that can be realised within our time'.[40]

The Labour Party was also just beginning to develop its wartime policies. On 23 May 1941 the NEC decided to form a special Committee on Post-war Economic and Social Reconstruction.[41] This spawned thirteen sub-committees including the Central Committee on Reconstruction Problems, chaired by Emmanuel Shinwell and with Harold Laski as its secretary. Controlled by a few prominent individuals, and particularly by Herbert Morrison, this committee and its sub-committees presented their views to the Labour Party Conferences and eventually in Labour's *Let Us Face the Future*, the general election manifesto of 1945.

These policies and expectations were given a boost by the fact that Clement Attlee was, effectively, Deputy Prime Minister throughout the period of the Churchill Coalition government. It fell to Attlee and Bevin to provide what became known as 'War Socialism'. Health and housing provision emerged, cheap school meals were made available for all school children and the war economy was regulated. Ernest Bevin, Minister of Labour, took powers to control the movement of Labour through the Essential Works Order (March 1941). Under this legislation, workers could be prevented from leaving jobs. Bevin was given the powers to direct labour, and he encouraged trade-union recognition and collective bargaining.

In many respects these were simply piecemeal responses to the wartime situation, a fact which was revealed in the debate over the Beveridge Report of 1942, *Social Insurance and Allied Services*.[42] This was a comprehensive scheme that gave systematic shape to the ideas on social security which was to be reorganized to provide a national minimum income, although it was to be dependent upon a national health service, family allowances and full employment. Churchill was suspicious about where such demands might lead but Attlee saw the Beveridge Report as an opportunity to introduce socialism.

Attlee emphasized the point when he said that 'Socialism does not admit to an alternative, Social Security to us can only mean Socialism.'[43] To Attlee, and his supporters, it was essential that the Beveridge Report should be quickly accepted as a vital commitment by the government. Yet it was quite clear that Churchill intended to delay its publication, and Attlee even felt that it might be saved until the end of the war to form part of the Conservative programme. Attlee was also hostile to the Churchill memorandum sent round government circles in which it was suggested that the economics of life might be such as to force a choice 'between social insurance and other urgent claims on limited resources'. Attlee sent in a counter-memorandum to the government urging that 'decisions must be taken and implemented in the field of post-war reconstruction *before* the end of the war'.[44] Churchill relented and the government accepted most of the report but gave the impression that it was committed to nothing. A Labour resolution that the government should support the Beveridge Report and implement it was defeated by 335 votes to 119, but 97 Labour MPs had voted against the government, 30 had abstained and only 23 had voted with the government, 22 of these being government ministers.

It is obvious that the Beveridge Report was a sensitive document, especially after the midsummer Gallup polls in 1943 when Labour registered a lead of 11 per cent over the Conservatives.[45] In the end the government was forced to set up a Reconstruction Committee towards the end of 1943, which developed the scheme that became the 1944 Education Act.[46] In 1944 the Reconstruction Committee put forward a scheme, which gained White Paper status, for guaranteeing 'Full Employment' through state action on Keynesian lines once large-scale unemployment occurred. Ernest Bevin moved its adoption by Parliament in June 1944 and found himself opposed by Aneurin Bevan who felt that it was simply a device for propping up capitalism and that socialism alone was the cure for unemployment.[47] Hugh Dalton was barely less critical, constantly referring to the vanity of Beveridge and the 'Beveridge muddle' in his diary.[48]

By 1945 the Labour Party was demonstrably the party most likely to introduce the social reforms that were essential if Britain was to avoid the economic and social mistakes of the interwar years. It won the general election in July 1945, called within two months of the end of the European war, by a substantial majority, with 393 seats against the Conservative Party's 213. The Liberals gained only 12 seats. Clement Attlee's Labour government had come to power.

CONCLUSION

Between 1931 and 1945 the Labour Party had improved its organization and sedulously developed its statist views. By 1935 it had recovered almost all the votes it had lost in 1931, if not its parliamentary position in the face of the National government. Indeed, at the 1935 Labour Party Conference, Jennie Adamson, only the second woman to act as Chairman, reflected that 'Labour now constitutes a formidable opposition in the House of Commons.'[49] Ten years later, Labour won its famous landslide general election victory. The intervening period had seen Labour wrestle with the problem of fascism and gain experience in a wartime government. Indeed, wartime Gallup polls provided continuing evidence of Labour's popularity with the electorate.

The Second World War had, quite clearly, provided the final push to Labour's success. Paul Addison has noted that wartime conditions did alter the context of debate: 'Had they [the Labour Party] gone to the country in 1939 with the programme of 1945, they would have been issuing a strongly radical challenge. But, in 1945, they had only to consolidate and extend the consensus achieved under the Coalition and build upon the new foundation of popular opinion.'[50] Yet it should be realized that the platform for success was laid down in the 1930s. The electoral victory of 1945 was the culmination of years of sedulous hard work. Yet it also provided the Labour Party with a serious challenge, as it was now faced with demonstrating that it was capable of implementing its socialist programme – a programme to meet the social optimism which had helped to sweep it to power in 1945. The real question, however, was whether Labour was ahead of or in tune with the demands of the electorate between 1945 and 1951.

CHAPTER FIVE

The High Point of Labour: the Attlee Governments, 1945–51

The two Attlee Labour governments of 1945 to 1951 can be viewed as high points in Labour's century of political progress. The first one, from 1945 to 1950, saw the development of the modern British welfare state, with the National Health Service as its coping stone. It also initiated the moves towards nationalization, which led to the public ownership of more than 20 per cent of the British economy, including mines and railways. Certainly the Attlee Labour governments were among the most active of peacetime British governments in the twentieth century. It is thus not surprising that their leading political figures[1] and their history[2] have been the subject of several important books. Many writers have tended to treat the Attlee years with respect, viewing them variously as evidence of planned socialism, of the shift to the left, or of the working out of Liberal policies forged in the 1930s and the Second World War. Indeed, some critics have implied that Labour's socialist programme owed much to wartime radicalism and planning and relatively little to the genuine demands from Labour politicians to introduce socialism.[3] Yet anyone examining the history of these governments has to acknowledge the immense importance of the Labour leadership in reshaping British society.

LABOUR'S VICTORY AND EXPECTATIONS

The young Hugh Gaitskell began his diary on 6 August 1945 by writing that 'It had been an extraordinary 10 days.'[4] Indeed, it had been so, for the Labour Party had won a landslide victory on 2 July, with 393 MPs (48 per cent of the poll) to the Conservatives' 213 MPs (39.6 per cent of the poll). It enjoyed a majority of 146 over the other political parties and Clement Attlee had no hesitation in accepting the King's commission to form a government. A Cabinet was formed and rank-and-file expectations were high that it would be able to introduce the programme of social welfare and nationalization which it had envisaged over the previous decade and in its electoral programme *Let Us Face the Future*. Yet if the socialist dawn had arrived in political terms it is clear that some of Labour's leading figures were, initially, doubtful of the new government's ability to deliver its socialist programme.

Within days of the Labour victory Hugh Dalton, the new Chancellor of the Exchequer, had called an informal meeting with some of the young but aspiring men of the Party, including Harold Wilson, Hugh Gaitskell, Richard Crossman, George Brown and John Freeman. Its purpose was to discuss the 'future policies and problems' of the Labour government. One of those present expressed the view that 'too many people had voted Labour in the hope that it means more pay and less work'.[5] Another spoke of the major problems of food, homes and fuel which would be 'extraordinarily difficult to handle at any rate in the first two years. It was, therefore, necessary that there should be full first-class publicity to make it clear that these difficulties were inevitable and inherited by the Labour government.'[6] Such fears were well founded because the new Labour government faced enormous economic difficulties.

During the Second World War British industry had been converted to war production at the cost of exports, facilitated by loans from the United States and the sale of British overseas assets. The result was that Britain's invisible earnings declined and that her visible exports were reduced to about one-third of their pre-war level. The Labour government's first priority was thus to secure financial support, which could only come from the United States, in order to buy food and raw materials while she was building up her export industries. The sudden end of the United States' 'lend-lease aid', which had been provided to Britain during the Second World War, in August 1945 exposed the weakness of the British economy and forced the British government to send John Maynard Keynes to the USA to secure a new loan. However, the final conditions of the loans were harsh, for Britain was expected to remove exchange controls and to make sterling freely convertible, with other currencies, within a year of taking up the loan. In fact, when Britain attempted to honour this agreement in July 1947 the economy was still too weak to withstand such a change of policy, and the Labour government was soon forced to reintroduce exchange controls. The continued fragility of the economy was further revealed by the balance of payments crisis in 1949, which occurred despite the fact that Britain's exports had increased by 60 per cent since 1945. And matters were not helped by a variety of setbacks over which the government had little control – most notably the severe winter of 1946/7, which led to coal shortages, the closure of factories and a temporary increase of unemployment to 2 million.

The British reliance upon American aid, and particularly the Americans' postwar Marshall Aid programme, tightened the link between the United States and Britain. Inevitably, there were political consequences. Indeed, Attlee and Bevin have often been criticized for their almost slavish acceptance of the alliance with the United States against the Soviet Union. This was certainly evident in the fact that Bevin helped forge the North Atlantic Treaty Organization (NATO), which came into existence in 1949 as an alliance of Western powers committed to countering the political threat and aggression of the Soviet Union. But this link was also apparent before in the way in which Bevin constantly referred to the 'special relationship' between Britain and the USA. It was also evident in the support which Britain showed towards the neo-fascist government of the Shah of Iran in the face of the Soviet threat to Britain's sources of oil in the Middle East. It might also be remembered that Attlee was one of the most anti-Soviet ministers in the wartime Coalition. Britain's pro-American and anti-Soviet policy in foreign affairs accorded with the sympathies of some of the leading members of the Labour Cabinet, though such policies owed much to the immense economic problems she faced in the postwar world.

THE WELFARE STATE – A LEGACY OF THE WAR?

Despite horrific and frightening economic problems, the first Labour government was able to extend greatly the responsibilities of the state during its early years in office. Although associated with nationalization, its greatest claim to fame is that it created the modern British welfare state. The Labour Party manifesto of 1950 proclaimed that 'Labour had honoured the pledge to make social security the birthright of every citizen. Today destitution has been banished. The best medical care is available to everybody in the land.'[7] Allowing for the natural exuberance of a party manifesto, the claims were largely true.

There is little doubt that Labour's social welfare programme would not have been possible without the American loan which provided the financial flexibility essential for the expansion of social provision. Yet

Labour could lay claim to some of the most detailed welfare planning before the Second World War, which such finance made possible. It had, as we have seen, built up its social welfare policies during the mid-1930s and, in 1937, had issued *Labour's Immediate Programme*, written by Dalton, which advanced schemes for social welfare and the creation of full employment. The Party's programme was presented to the electorate in the Party's *Let Us Face the Future*, published in 1945. Both documents made vague reference to the need for a National Health Service, national insurance, and a house-building programme. Although specific detailed programmes were thin, it was widely assumed that the Labour Party would be the one likely to introduce comprehensive welfare measures. Its wartime experience in government made that an increased possibility, as did the support it gave to the Beveridge Report of 1942, which would have been shelved by Winston Churchill, the Prime Minister, had there been no Labour pressure for it.

The Beveridge Report was an important aspect of the Attlee government's immediate postwar policy. James Griffiths, the minister responsible for National Insurance, was intent on applying the Beveridge Report and introduced a scheme to Parliament along similar lines in 1946, to be implemented in 1948, committed to the principle of providing a 'National Minimum Standard'. Sick benefits, unemployment benefits, family allowances, maternity and widows' benefits were introduced. There were minor differences compared with the Beveridge Report, and there was an element of means testing, but to all intents and purposes the Labour government proved to be a faithful advocate of Beveridge's scheme – of which it had been part instigator.

Nevertheless, there was no straight line of ideas from the Beveridge Report to the postwar Labour government's welfare state. The link with the National Insurance Act of 1946 (introduced in 1948) was clear but that is as far as it went. The National Health Service Act of 1946 (introduced in 1948) owed very little to Beveridge.

The Beveridge Report advocated the introduction of a comprehensive health and rehabilitation service and emphasized the need for a universal and contributory scheme of health provision which would make medical and dental treatment immediately available whether in private or public health hospitals. There was an assumption, however, that contemporary provision of private and public health provision might be better organized. The Labour Party and the wartime government more or less accepted such ideas during the war. But none of their reports and schemes ever envisaged the nationalization of the hospitals which Aneurin (Nye) Bevan's National Health Service Act intended, nor the extent to which Bevan's scheme contemplated GPs being drawn into the NHS on a partly salaried basis. The fact is that Nye Bevan's National Health Service Act went much further than the Beveridge Report had suggested. Bevan's NHS scheme was innovative and, in contrast to the Beveridge scheme, not based upon personal contributions. The National Insurance Act provided a contributory sickness benefit scheme but it did not pay for the National Health Service, only for the loss of earnings of the sick. The NHS, as such, was paid for out of taxation.

The passing of the National Health Service Act in 1946 and its introduction in 1948 were, of course, accompanied by a tremendous outburst of opposition. In the first place, Herbert Morrison, Lord President of the Council (effectively Deputy Prime Minister), opposed its introduction in Cabinet on the basis that, quite correctly, it was not in the Labour Party's election manifesto. Bevan soon overcame this opposition to be faced with a more serious challenge from the British Medical Association (BMA). It objected, among other things, to the GPs becoming part civil servants, in the sense that they were to be paid partly by the state, it wished to protect the right of doctors to sell their practices, and opposed the threat of their being sent to 'under-doctored' areas. Eventually, after much argument and opposition during which Bevan condemned the Tory supporters of the BMA as being 'lower than vermin' – a statement which led them to form 'vermin clubs' throughout the country – and BMA votes and referendums against the NHS, the doctors flocked over to the NHS once it was officially formed in July 1948. Yet the cost of it rose from an initial estimate of £128 million in the first year to a figure in excess of £278 million. Even Bevan was alarmed at the high level of expenditure involved. Moreover, it was estimated that the cost might rise to £356 million in its second year of operation and there was staunch resistance to it from Herbert Morrison and Sir Stafford Cripps, the new Chancellor of the Exchequer, who were pressing both for the curbing of expenditure and for prescription charges.[8] Aware that there was pressure for these amendments from within the Cabinet, Nye Bevan announced, at a Labour rally in Staffordshire on 25 September 1949, that there was no inclination to curb expenditure and that 'I have made up my mind that the National Health Service is not going to be touched, and there is no disposition by the Government to touch it . . . the health service is sacrosanct.'[9] The majority of the Cabinet disagreed and pressed for the control of health expenditure. This apparently intractable issue was resolved only when Bevan was later moved from the Ministry of Health to the Ministry of Labour, following Labour's victory in the 1950 general election. However, he resigned from the Labour government in April 1951, in protest at the intended introduction of prescription charges, taking with him the Labour left or 'Bevanites'. Nevertheless, despite the problems that arose, it is clear that the NHS was a success. Bevan could rightly stress, with a certain amount of pride, that the 'National Health Service and the welfare state have come to be used as interchangeable terms. . . .'[10]

Labour's welfare state also introduced legislation to improve housing, pay family allowances, provide benefits for those suffering injuries and offer national assistance to those who did not have the right to claims benefited under the Industrial Insurance Act of 1946. Most of this was in place by early July 1948 when, effectively, Labour's modern welfare state, based upon a system of universal, but low, benefits and provisions, began to function as a low-cost social security system.

NATIONALIZATION AND LABOUR'S COMMITMENT TO SOCIALISM

The most serious doubts about the Labour government's commitment to socialism, and the redistribution of wealth and income in Britain, arose from its plan for the 'socialization of industry'. Although the government moved quickly to nationalize both services and industry it has been argued that it had little compunction to go further than those measures which were deemed to be absolutely essential in order to redeem its political pledges and to improve the efficiency of the economy. The diffident attitude of Attlee towards the whole process of public control and the modest and vacillating conviction of Herbert Morrison did little to assure the left wing of the Party that public ownership would ever be used as a weapon of regulation and control for the whole economy. The slowdown of the public ownership programme from 1948, following the nationalization of coal mines, railways and other industries and services, convinced the Labour left that the government lacked a firm-rooted commitment to socialist planning and control. (The organization and policies of the Labour left are discussed later in this chapter.)

In spite of pressure from the Labour left, Attlee's Labour governments lacked a clearly thought-out strategy for public ownership. Before and during the war, the Party had discussed and revised the list of industries and services due for nationalization but had invariably failed to draw up detailed plans and schemes. Emmanuel Shinwell, as Minister of Fuel and Power in 1945, was given to reflect that

> I had believed, as other members had, that in the Party archives a blueprint was ready. Now, as Minister of Fuel and Power, I found that nothing practical and tangible existed. There were some pamphlets, some memoranda produced for private circulation, and nothing else. I had to start with a clear desk.[11]

This was an exaggeration, even though it did reveal the intellectual void at the centre of Labour's proposals for nationalization.

Hugh Dalton's work in the 1930s and Herbert Morrison's nationalization list in *Let Us Face the Future* were the only plans on offer. Yet there was no commitment to link the nationalized industries and services into some grand strategy for an assault on the bastions of capitalism. Nevertheless, the Labour government, in its rush to fulfil its pledge to nationalize, moved quickly. The Bank of England, civil aviation, and cable and wireless were nationalized in 1946; railways, transport and electricity in 1947; gas in 1948 and the early measures for iron and steel in 1948 and 1949. The bulk of the activity occurred between 1945 and 1947.

Much of this early programme of nationalization caused little controversy, although the shortage of coal in the bad winter of 1946/7 led to some criticism of the National Coal Board. However, the later programme of nationalization caused increasing problems. There was fierce Conservative opposition to the Transport Act of 1947, which nationalized both the railways and road haulage, and also against the 1948 Gas Act. In the case of the latter, the Conservative opposition produced over 800 amendments to it before it was forced through Parliament.

Up to a point, then, the Labour government had revealed its resolve, if not its coherence, in approaching matters of public ownership. Quite clearly, each bill was treated as a separate measure and the whole strategy of public ownership was confined to the industries and services involved. Such fragmentation of approach was evident in the case of the nationalization of iron and steel.

The Labour Party had been reluctant to demand the nationalization of iron and steel until forced to do so by Ian Mikardo's intervention at the

1944 Labour Party Conference which added it to the list for nationalization, much against the wishes of Herbert Morrison. The fact is that Morrison had always been opposed to the proposal, and support for his reluctance increased in the economic and financial chaos of 1947. By that time the majority of the Labour Cabinet favoured either its deferment or its abandonment. Yet it was pushed through, perhaps because of the commitment to nationalization and to appease Nye Bevan, in the face of hostile steel manufacturers, a determined opposition and a stubbornly obstinate House of Lords. The industry was eventually nationalized in 1950, although subsequently denationalized by the next Conservative government.

By 1950–1, the government was reluctant to nationalize any more industries. They now had control of around 20 per cent of the economy. To many in the Party, nationalization had been the justification for Labour taking office. It was evidence, even more than the welfare state, that Labour was willing to introduce socialism. If the Labour government lost its way and had no clear comprehension of how to use what was, to the Party, this symbol of socialism that did not make its efforts less worthwhile. They did at least attempt to take the country in a socialist direction in domestic affairs. It is less obvious that they attempted to do this in foreign affairs.

FOREIGN AFFAIRS, THE COMMONWEALTH AND DEFENCE

In the immediate postwar years it was widely expected that a Labour government would be committed to the policies of disarmament and international reconciliation which it had advocated for most of the inter-war years. It was further expected that it would preside over the end of colonial rule and the creation of the newly emerged Commonwealth. By the late 1940s there was no longer an illusion that Labour would implement the peace policies of the past, though there was a sense of satisfaction at the fact that Britain was disengaging from Empire and had, under difficult circumstances, created the independent new Commonwealth states of India and Pakistan.

There is no doubt that Attlee's government moved from a commitment to a non-aggressive foreign policy to one of aggression, particularly against the Soviet Union. At the end of the Second World War there had been hopes of strengthening the ties with the Soviet Union but, in April

1949, the Washington Conference had fully confirmed the anti-Soviet attitude of the Labour government in its decision to form the North Atlantic Treaty Organization. Clearly, much had changed during the intervening four years.

Labour's switch to the right, and to the alliance with the United States against the Soviet Union, had been conditioned by many factors. The most obvious was the appointment of Ernest Bevin as Foreign Secretary, though the government's need of the American loan and its wariness of the pacific policies of the interwar years were contributory factors. Bevin brought with him a reputation of being something of an anti-communist largely due to his battles with Bert Papworth and the communist-led London busmen within in his own union, the Transport and General Workers' Union. During the Second World War he held few illusions about the difficulties which would be faced in dealing with the Soviet Union in the postwar world. He was confirmed in his own fears when he found the Russians reluctant to agree to the reunification of Germany, imposing the blockade on Berlin and criticizing Britain's policies in the Middle East.[12]

Bevin was also aware of the need to avoid a repeat of the interwar years, when the United States adopted an isolationist policy. The end of Lend-Lease, the process by which the USA provided Britain with the wartime equipment and goods she needed, raised memories of the USA's pre-war isolation and motivated him to strengthen the link with the USA in the context of Britain's need to negotiate an American loan and what he perceived to be the rising threat of the Soviet Union to Britain's interests in the Middle East and western Europe.

Bevin was still convinced that Britain was a major world power and that she was threatened by the Soviet Union. He had been prepared to work with the Soviet Union at the end of the war but his difficult dealings with the Russians forced him to conclude treaties with the French and other nations and to arrive at the view that Britain needed to maintain a military presence in 'West Germany'. He also publicly announced the idea of a 'Western Union' in the House of Commons on 23 January 1948. This was at a time of Soviet expansion in eastern Europe and Bevin concluded that western Europe would have to consider ways in which to protect itself. From that point onwards Bevin sought to get the United States involved in the 'Western Union' but was rejected by the Americans. However, the communist coup in Czechoslovakia on 5 March 1948, and the blockade of Berlin in the summer of 1948, changed matters. The blockade of Berlin, whereby the Russians cut off the rail and road links between Berlin and the West and ended the supply of electricity to the western sector of the city from the Soviet sector and the eastern zone, led to the Berlin airlift, which involved American cooperation with Britain in order to maintain 'West' Berlin.

By the autumn of 1948, amid genuine fears that the western European nations would be overrun by the Russians in the event of war, there were clear signs that a Western Alliance was likely to be formed. The United States finally agreed to commit itself to the support of the western European nations at the Washington Conference on 4 April 1949, after protracted and intense discussions. As Bevin signed the NATO agreement he commented that:

> I am doing so on behalf of a free and ancient parliamentary nation and I am satisfied that the step we are taking has the almost unanimous approval of the British people. . . .
>
> Our people do not want and do not glorify war, but they will not shrink from it if aggression is threatened.[13]

Nevertheless, it must not be assumed that Britain was slavish in her support of the United States. There were, in fact, many points of disagreement on international matters. The United States did not, for instance, favour other nations sharing in the development of the atomic bomb and so Attlee committed Britain to developing an independent atomic capability. There were also many other points of departure, none more obvious than the events in Palestine.

Ever since the Balfour Declaration of 1917 Britain had been committed to a 'national home for the Jewish people', although this intent had always been tempered by the desire to protect the interests of the non-Jewish communities. It soon became obvious that these joint objectives were not possible. The flood of Jewish immigrants into Palestine during the 1930s was too much for the Arab community and too little for the Jews. While various interwar governments attempted to regulate the flow of immigration it appeared that the Labour Party favoured Jewish immigration more than it feared Arab reaction. Poale Zion, the Jewish Labour Party, was affiliated to the Labour Party and Jewish Labour MPs, such as Emmanuel (Manny) Shinwell and Lewis Silkin, campaigned strongly to win Labour support for the creation of an independent Jewish state. Thus it is not surprising that the Labour Party Conference of 1944 strongly associated itself with the continued Jewish immigration into

Palestine and the gradual withdrawal of the Arab community. Yet neither Ernest Bevin nor the Labour government pursued such a line when in power and responsible for the administration of Palestine.

From the start Bevin adopted a more even-handed approach, which did not please President Truman, and the United States, who demanded the immediate admission of 100,000 Jews into Palestine in 1945. The Palestine Committee of the British Cabinet limited Jewish immigration to 1,500 per month, although it was agreed that an Anglo-American Commission would be set up to examine the issues involved. Even though it confirmed the need to admit 100,000 Jews, Attlee refused to accept the recommendation without an agreement to reduce the size of the military forces being mustered by both the Jews and the Arabs. From the start, British and American interests were at odds, a situation which was not helped by Ernest Bevin's cutting remark that 'they [the Americans] did not want too many Jews in New York'.[14]

Bevin's acrimonious outburst did not endear him to the Americans and, eventually, the continued illegal immigration of the Jews, the naval blockade and the infamous episode of the ship *Exodus*, violence against British troops, the United Nations Committee and its advocacy of the partition of Palestine into Jewish and Arab states, and the civil war, forced Bevin to allow the creation of the state of Israel in January 1949 and led to the ignominious withdrawal of British troops.

Yet despite Bevin's attempted even-handedness on Palestine, it cannot be denied that the Labour government's foreign policy lacked a clear socialist perspective. For instance, the fear of communism and the need to identify with the USA for financial reasons saw Britain support the United States in its actions over the Korean War.

In the case of India, however, Labour's response was more in line with what was expected. Attlee, and other Labour politicians, had indicated their intention to offer some measure of independence to India before the Second World War. Attlee now sent a delegation of Cabinet ministers to India in February 1946 to conduct intricate negotiations with the Congress and the Muslim leaders. They found no consensus and were forced to produce a complex three-tier system of government which ruled out the idea of creating the state of Pakistan. As a result an interim government was formed under Pandit Nehru, in September 1946. Yet the rising level of violence between the Hindus and the Muslims threatened its continued existence and provoked the Viceroy, Lord Mountbatten, to bring forward the withdrawal of British troops to 15 August 1947 – the day on which the Indian Congress agreed that India and Pakistan would formally become independent states, and full members of the Commonwealth. The occasion was marred by widespread bloodshed throughout India. It is possible that the end of the British Raj could have been handled more effectively, though doubtful given the contending forces in play.

The Labour government was clearly deflected from part of the political course which it aimed to pave in 1945. Its foreign policy conditioned by a variety of events, was never to be the socialist policy which many of its supporters had hoped for, though there was some credit to be drawn from its actions in India and Palestine. But this aberrant foreign policy was partly conditioned by Britain's postwar economic problems, many of which would have been insurmountable without the American loan.

THE FINANCIAL CRISES

The driving force behind the actions of the Labour government was the need for financial stability, without which there could have been no significant progress towards socialism. In the first instance, financial stability was provided by the American loan. Later, the Marshall Aid programme, offering American aid to Europe, provided the Labour government with the means to introduce its social legislation between 1945 and 1947. The decision to make the pound sterling convertible with the dollar (dollars would be paid for pounds on request) on 15 July 1947, a condition of the loan, paved the way for a change in direction in the economic and social programme of the Labour government.

As Attlee's first Chancellor of the Exchequer, Hugh Dalton had pursued economic policies which had sought expansion rather than deflation. The American loan had provided him with the resources to pay for nationalization, the recovery of house building and the whole panoply of social reform. But in 1947 matters began to go wrong. The fuel crisis and coal shortage, resulting from the bad winter of 1946/7, destroyed the conviction that socialist planning could cope with any situation and there was a temporary rise of unemployment to about 2 million. Imposed upon this evident failure of planning was the sharp rise in American prices in 1947, which undermined the value of the American loan, contributed to the balance of payments crisis of the summer and the constant dollar drain from the British gold and currency

*The Independent Labour Council, 1899. With the sections of the trade union movement, the
Independent Labour Council formed the Labour Representation Committee on 27 February 1900.
Back row, left to right: J.R. MacDonald, Joseph Burgess, James Parker, John Penny and France
Littlewood. Front row: J. Bruce Glasier, James Keir Hardie, H. Russell Smart and Philip Snowden.
(All pictures reproduced by permission of the National Museum of Labour History)*

*Memorial Hall, Farringdon Street, London,
the birthplace of the Labour Representation
Committee (Labour Party) on 27 February
1900.*

James Keir Hardie addressing a meeting attended by Philip Snowden (far left), c. 1910.

James Keir Hardie, Mrs Bernard Shaw, Revd Geoffrey Ramsay and George Bernard Shaw at Merthyr Tydfil during one of the 1910 general election contests.

James Ramsay MacDonald, the first Secretary of the Labour Party, 1907.

*George Lansbury, briefly leader of the Labour
Party in the early 1930s after the defection of
J.R. MacDonald, c. 1910.*

*Edward Bellamy, the American author of
the socialist novel* Looking Backwards,
G.J. Wardle, editor of the Railway
Times, *and Arthur Henderson, c. 1920.*

James Ramsay MacDonald and Arthur Henderson, c. 1922.

Labour's first Cabinet, 1924. On the front row, Philip Snowden, Chancellor of the Exchequer, is third from the left, J.R. MacDonald is fifth from the left, J.R. Clynes is sixth from the left, J.H. Thomas is seventh from the left and Arthur Henderson is on the extreme right.

The Labour Cabinet, 1929. J.H. Thomas, Philip Snowden, J.R. MacDonald, Arthur Henderson and Sidney Webb, are sat between the third and seventh positions from the left on the front row.

The Cabinet of the National government of 1931, which included Philip Snowden (front row, first left) and Ramsay MacDonald (front row, third left and seated next to Stanley Baldwin) and J.H. Thomas (second from the left on the back row).

The young Barbara Castle (Barbara Betts), early 1930s.

reserves. By the summer of 1947 more than half of the arranged loan of $3,750 million, which was supposed to last until 1951, was gone and it appeared that the rest would go in 1948. In such circumstances the decision to make the pound convertible was a foolish step, though an inevitable one if the government was to honour the pledge. The result was a financial disaster and the run on the pound was so heavy that the government was forced to impose a temporary suspension of convertibility on 20 August 1947. This became permanent in December 1947.

This financial mistake changed the whole course of the Labour government's approach to the economy. Within a few months Dalton was replaced as Chancellor of the Exchequer by Sir Stafford Cripps. With this change came new austerity measures coupled with a new export drive. The economy was greatly strengthened by this action and the devaluation of the pound in 1949 gave a stimulus to exports.

Despite its problems, the Attlee government had brought about a major growth in the economy. In 1949 industrial production in Britain was about 30 per cent above that of 1938 and between 1945 and 1949 the value of exports had risen from 50 per cent of the pre-war level to almost 55 per cent above. Nevertheless, the economic problems effectively brought Labour's nationalization programme to an end and Hugh Dalton and Herbert Morrison moved towards 'consolidation', rather than a new programme of nationalization.

'THE SALUTARY GADFLY' AND THE 'LOST SHEEP': KEEP LEFT AND THE LABOUR LEFT 1945–51

There was a rather amorphous body of opinion emerging in these years which is associated with the Labour left. It emerged, in fragmented form, advocated by several small political groupings who were often in conflict with one another. The moderate or 'soft' left tended to accrete to the Keep Left Group, which later became the Bevanites and Tribunites, associated with *Tribune* or Aneurin Bevan. The 'hard' Labour left was small and equally divided into groups whose unity began to diminish from 1947 onwards. It included MPs such as Konni Zilliacus (MP for Gateshead, later Gateshead East), Geoffrey Bing (Hornchurch), J.F. Platts Mills (Finsbury), Leslie Solley (Thurrock) and Leslie Hutchinson (Manchester, Rusholme). Most of these were expelled from the Labour Party in 1949 and helped form the Labour Independent Group. From time to time, those of the 'hard' and 'soft' left found themselves in other socialist groupings such as Victory for Socialism, the Europe Group (formed by eighty MPs in 1947) and numerous small and temporary associations that developed within the Labour Party.

As they emerged, these Labour left groups, ten in number by 1952, tended to adopt rather different attitudes towards the Labour Party, particularly with regard to foreign policy and the domestic economic situation. The Keep Left Group of MPs, organized by Ian Mikardo, affectionately known as 'Mik', Richard Crossman, and others, tended to accept the view that a third world war could only be avoided by the creation of a 'Third Force', based upon an alliance between Britain and France and wider European support, which would encourage disarmament and the use of the money saved to develop the economies of the Third World, and thus the prosperity, through trading, of the industrial world.[15] This view contrasted sharply with that put forward by *Tribune* (a left-wing journal first published in 1937 which by the late 1940s was dropping some of its extreme left-wing opposition to the British link with the United States) and evident when Mikardo left the editorial board of that paper in May 1949. Prompted by Mikardo's departure, Michael Foot provided a highly reasoned article justifying the House of Commons' endorsement of the Atlantic Pact (NATO) and explaining why the democratically oriented USA was more to be trusted than the far more totalitarian USSR. He wrote that

> Whatever follies have been committed by American policy since 1945 (and they are manifold) the major purpose and the major result has been to provide aid without which recovery from the war would have been infinitely more arduous. The major purpose of Soviet policy has been the complete subjugation of as many countries as possible to Soviet will. . . . There is a difference worth noting between the offer of dollars to Governments, including Socialist ones, by the United States and the provision of concentration camps and execution squads for the victims, including Soviet victims, of Soviet Communism.[16]

Foot suggested, to Ian Mikardo, that it was highly unlikely that had Britain adopted a more socialist policy, or the 'Third Force' policy, that Stalin would have taken any notice at all or allowed democratic elections in Poland. Indeed, 'The Czech socialists and all the Czech parties had taken precisely those actions of seeking accommodation with the

Russians which Ian Mikardo seems to prescribe. None of them were sufficient to save them from annihilation. Neither they nor Marshal Tito were to be allowed the exercise of any scope of independence.'

Keep Left began as a small group of friends, all MPs, who began to nurture a particular and distinctive political outlook. There were about fifteen of them and they met on a regular but informal basis. The leading figures were Richard Crossman, Ian Mikardo and Michael Foot. They all had distinguished left-wing credentials; Mikardo had presented the motion which committed the next Labour government to nationalization at the Labour Party Conference in 1944. Crossman had also been troublesome to the Labour government, producing the amendment to the King's Speech in December 1946, which demanded that the Labour government should

> so renew and recast its conduct of international affairs as to affirm the utmost encouragement to and collaboration with all nations striving to secure full Socialist planning and control of the world's resources, and thus provide a democratic and constructive Socialist alternative to an otherwise inevitable conflict between American capitalism and Soviet Communism in which all hope of world Government would be destroyed.[17]

This amendment reflected some of the later views of the Keep Left Group but was defeated easily. Foot was an editor of *Tribune* and later, in the early 1980s, became the Leader of the Labour Party.

The Keep Left Group met, on an informal basis, regularly during the bad winter of 1947 and, in May, produced a 47-page pamphlet, *Keep Left*, mainly written by Michael Foot, Ian Mikardo and Richard Crossman. It congratulated the Labour government on its domestic achievements but suggested that it needed to extend nationalization and plan the development of the economy more effectively through the creation of a Ministry of Economic Affairs and joint production committees to win the 'Battle for Production'. Yet it felt that such domestic planning and growth could not be achieved without a balanced foreign policy. Crossman, who wrote the foreign policy section, suggested that the USA and the USSR were equally responsible for the development of two hostile blocs and suggested that a socialist Britain could not prosper without the gradual creation of some kind of unity between European nations, the vast majority of whom were planning their economy on socialist lines. Crossman stressed that Britain should start by developing economic and military relations with France and that 'We should try to expand the Anglo-French Alliance into a European security pact' and renounce atomic armaments and war.[18] Emphasis was placed upon the creation of a 'regional European Security System' that would effectively act as a 'Third Force', independent of the USA and the USSR but designed to bring the two super powers closer together.[19] There was also the implication, though not fully spelled out at this stage, that the British armed forces, and those of other nations, would be reduced and that the African colonies could be economically developed to help Britain maintain her economic independence of the United States.[20]

This pamphlet was the basis of the Keep Left approach. The subsidiary idea, of developing the undeveloped or Third World economies from the savings of disarmament, was further evident in Fenner Brockway's report on his 40-minute meeting with Pandit Nehru on 20 September 1950. Brockway, an established left-wing journalist, sometime member of the Independent Labour Party and the Labour Party, was associated with the ideas of Keep Left at this time, although he could not attend its meetings as of right since he was not a Labour MP until the 1950 general election. At his meeting with Nehru, he proposed 'that an offer should be made by one or more of the Western powers to direct expenditure on armaments to a World Plan for lifting the standards of life of the people. . . .'[21] Brockway also discussed the need to keep open negotiations with China. Nehru felt that the 'World Plan proposal is important but should be put forward at a more suitable psychological moment than at the present' and that the Labour left ought to pressure the British government to restrain the USA and keep the door open for negotiations with China, at a time when the Korean War was waging.

Keep Left was produced at a vital moment in the life of the first Attlee government. Within three months of its emergence the Labour government had announced large expenditure cuts at a time when the American loan was ending. This provoked nineteen Labour MPs, including the fifteen who had signed *Keep Left* and James Callaghan (Cardiff South), a later Leader of the Labour Party and Prime Minister, to send a letter to the *Daily Herald*, indicating the need for alternative acts and new strategies. They proposed that the armed forces should be cut further, that there needed to be equality of sacrifice, that Britain should develop further her trading links and that socialist planning was required to 'secure mass production'.[22] The subsequent debate suggested that cuts of £225 million were not enough and that an expansion of production was necessary.[23] *Keep Left*, with its fight for production and socialist planning, seemed very appropriate at this time.

Despite all the efforts of Keep Left, including its reaction against the Czechoslovakian crisis which saw the death of its beloved example of democratic socialism, one must recognize that it was a small group of a dozen to twenty MPs. There were divisions which often undermined their unity, most particularly when in May 1949, due to varying attitudes towards the Atlantic Pact, Michael Foot was detached from Keep Left activities and Ian Mikardo left the editorial board of *Tribune*.[24] It was in the wake of these changes in attitude by some of its members that the group decided to come into official existence.

Keep Left was formed officially on 25 July 1949, in order to examine the international peace situation and to put forward its views to the Labour Party.[25] There were thirteen members present at the first meeting – including Barbara Castle, Richard Crossman, Ian Mikardo and Leslie Hale. Mikardo was made a *pro tem* secretary and Leslie Hale, another Labour MP with prominent left-wing connections, was acting chairman. They invited economic advisers to the Group, including Tom Balogh, Professor of Economics at Oxford and, rather hopefully given their previous track record, decided to remain secret for a few months and that 'just before the resumption of the House the Group should make its existence publicly known by the issue of a statement'.[26]

The Keep Left Group was anxious to develop policies and to 'rewrite *Labour Believes in Britain* in terms of an extension of Keep Left'.[27] It re-emphasized that Britain's approach to the Americans should be 'a European rather than a narrowly British line',[28] and there was considerable discussion of the Keep Left policies already outlined. The Group raised the possibility of establishing national minimum wage levels, supporting the Schuman Plan for European Unity (the basis of the development to the modern European Economic Community), the reunification of Germany and the dangers of rearming Germany. Yet four issues began to dominate its debates from the beginning of 1950 – the Korean crisis, the dissemination of socialist ideas, the survival of the Group and the resignation of Aneurin Bevan.

The North Korean invasion of South Korea on 25 June 1950, when they marched across the 38th parallel, united the Labour left and the Keep Left Group behind the government. However, Keep Left was opposed to widening the war against mainland China and particularly condemned

General MacArthur's invasion of North Korea in November 1950 and opposed the British government sending land forces to Korea (MacArthur, an American, was still the Supreme Commander of the Allied Powers in Japan and the Far East).[29] There was also the wider concern that Britain had decided, under American pressure, to increase her defence budget to £4,700 million over three years (not the £700 million or 7.5 per cent of national income agreed for 1950–1).[30] This decision, provoked by the Korean War, had wider implications for the British economy since it meant that British domestic expenditure would have to be reduced. The Group also decided to extend *Keep Left* into *Keeping Left*, and to produce over forty 'Group Papers' and organize the left-wing Brains Trust throughout the country in order to heighten the awareness of socialist ideas. *Keeping Left* sold more than 30,000 copies in a few months,[31] and Mikardo, who was mainly responsible for the Brains Trust scheme (based on a discussion group touring the country), was involved in voluminous correspondence arranging the meetings.[32] The Brains Trust movement, in particular, caught on and became associated with the Tribune Group in the 1950s. Indeed, Crossman referred to an NEC meeting in 1953 when he recalled how it was said that 'the next logical thing to do is to examine the Tribune Brains Trust and see if they are a party within a party. Edith Summerskill, looking at Mikardo, 'who I think is the most hated Bevanite', suggested that suspected fellow travellers should be expelled.[33]

There is no doubting that the Keep Left Group was developing ideas but without numbers and influence they were never going to be of more than marginal importance. Indeed, the Group became increasingly concerned about its own preservation in 1950 and 1951, when the much reduced Labour majority at the 1950 general election raised the imminent prospect of another general election. There was also the concern that the membership of the Group seemed to be changing constantly and that there were still only twelve Group members at the end of 1949 and early 1950.[34] Thereafter, the Group gradually expanded, with Fenner Brockway, among others, joining the Group in March 1950.[35] This expansion was offset by resignations.[36]

By early 1951, the Group became more self-conscious of its own position. There were two reasons for this. Firstly, the resignation of Aneurin Bevan, Harold Wilson and John Freeman from the Labour government had quickly increased its membership. All three had joined the Group within three days of their resignations and encouraged others to do likewise.[37] By the end of 1951 there were at least forty-seven Group members and four others were considered attached.[38] Secondly, it was obvious that the Labour government's small parliamentary majority, in the face of a left-wing rebellion, was going to produce a general election. Accordingly, throughout 1951, the Group developed the idea of a 'Mutual Aid Scheme', whereby those Keep Left MPs in vulnerable seats were assisted in their campaign by other Keep Left MPs in safe seats.[39]

The general election of 1951 made relatively minor inroads into Keep Left, despite bringing about the defeat of the Labour Party, but it was clear that it brought about the end of the Group in the old form. The Labour left had become strong in the constituency Labour parties well before the famous 1952 Annual Conference, when it astonished Britain by electing six out of seven 'Bevanites' to the constituencies' section of the National Executive Committee.[40] The balance of power within the Labour Party's NEC had moved to the left and the Party was now, at least for three or four years, to be divided between the Bevanites, who demanded more social planning and nationalization, and the 'revisionists', such as Tony Crosland and Hugh Gaitskell (referred to in the next chapter), who were intent on abandoning nationalization and emphasizing the redistribution of income and wealth via taxation and increased social spending.

The message to Keep Left was clear for it now had to abandon 'its old functions of salutary gadfly and think in realistic terms of acquiring power'. It was suggested 'that the Group should no longer be small, hand-picked and self-appointed, black-balling its potential friends on this score or on that like a snob West End club and turning them if not into enemies, at least into critics'. It was hoped that it would be increased to at least a hundred members and that all members should bring in new ones with an argument along the lines of

> Listen, duckie, Keep Left has been during the last five or six years a small, haphazard Group, self-appointed on no particular principle, as always happens in these cases. We kept small for the practical reason that it was always hard for a large group to function. However, we would like you to join forces with us, as we suspect you to be socialistically inclined! So will you come along on such and such a date?[41]

It was argued that the widened Group would then form an Executive Committee of about twenty probably drawn largely from the existing members, and that all its adherents would be formed into small functional bodies of about ten or twelve members who would produce Group Papers on 'New Thinking on the nationalized Industries. A Revised Relationship with America. A Policy for the Middle East. A Socialist Attitude towards Private Industry. Trade Unions in the New Society. Etc.'[42] The main point was that the new widened Group would be active in developing, going beyond having a permanent minority status and ensuring that 'the majority we command among the rank and file is reflected inside the Parliamentary Party'.[43]

The activities of the Keep Left Group were important in preparing the ground for the 'Bevanites' in the early 1950s, although it was but one strand of that movement. The fierce internal strife within the Labour Party, that lasted from the major backbench revolt over rearmament in March 1952, when fifty-seven Labour MPs defied the Labour Whip and voted against the Conservative government's first Defence White Paper, until the eve of the 1955 general election owed much to this reshaped and extended Labour left grouping. The Bevanite Brains Trust, or Tribune Brains Trust, which toured the country pressing forward left-wing cases first emerged in the ranks of Keep Left. In addition, the petition of left-wing MPs of April 1954, which criticized the Conservative government for not meeting with the United States and the USSR to control and reduce the spread of the hydrogen bomb, owed its origins to Keep Left.[44]

Nevertheless, this outright opposition that Bevan presented in the mid-1950s went some way beyond what Keep Left was prepared to contemplate in the late 1940s. The moderate Labour left had always kept its distance from the 'hard' left – those who were considered to be closely connected with communism and the subject of the 'Lost Sheep' file of Morgan Phillips, secretary of the Labour Party – whereas Bevan was prepared to challenge the Labour Party much more directly and was almost expelled as a result.[45]

Only a small rump of MPs, who could be regarded as the 'hard' left, challenged the Labour leadership in the late 1940s as Bevan was to challenge it in the 1950s. They were quickly isolated by the Labour Party and were detached from the Keep Left Group. This small rump seems to have emerged on 27 March 1946, when Ernest Bevin demanded a vote of confidence from his party with regard to his foreign policy. Six Labour MPs voted against him. These were Konni Zilliacus, Elizabeth (Bessie) Braddock, Emrys Hughes, Julius Silverman, W. Warbey and Lyall Wilkes.

Some of them, particularly Braddock, Hughes and Silverman, gravitated to the 'soft' left position as events unfolded, and others on the fringe, like Tom Driberg, never quite maintained their 'hard' left credentials. Indeed, in the end it was Zilliacus plus Leslie Solley and John Platts Mills, both of whom had not been involved in the vote, who became the martyrs of the 'hard' left.[46] They presented pro-communist ideas on many occasions and were expelled from the Labour Party in 1948 and 1949.

Excluded from the Labour Party they formed the Labour Independent Group in 1949, with Konni Zilliacus, John Platts Mills, D.N. Pritt and Lester Hutchinson being the chief figures. They continued to press forward with the idea of working with the communists and were particularly caught up with the idea of Eurocommunism once Yugoslavia, under Tito, revealed its independence from Moscow in 1949. The Labour Independent Group also associated with the ill-fated Socialist Fellowship, which promoted international socialism, and the Victory for Socialism group which had first emerged in 1934 but failed constantly to gain significant support. The expelled Labour MPs found their influence much diminished and it is obvious, given that they posed little threat to the Labour Party leadership, that they were expelled as a warning to the 'soft' left not to step too far out of line.

Despite these constraints the Labour left, and particularly Keep Left, had made its contribution to the debate about the future of socialism in Britain. It offered loftier ideals than those set by the Labour Party. Indeed, of Keep Left, Ian Mikardo concluded:

> Unlike its successors, the Keep Left Group was concerned with the long term rather than the immediate. The agendas of the later Bevanite and Tribune Group meetings were and are dominated by the week's business in the House and other current or imminent issues, but in Keep Left the greater part of our discussions was about the basic philosophy of the Party and the sort of broad economic and social order we should be seeking to create. Between 1947 and 1950 we concentrated on the production of a wide-ranging programme for the next Labour government. . . .[47]

THE END OF THE ATTLEE YEARS

By 1950 the Labour government was clearly in difficulty. It had achieved its main legislative thrust in the immediate postwar years and the electorate was less supportive of it in the 1950 general election. The Labour government's initiative was further stifled by the financial difficulties it faced, most notably the rapidly rising costs which Britain's involvement in the Korean War added to the defence bill. In addition, the trade unions were no longer prepared to control wage demands as they had been willing to do in the early years of the Attlee administration. For its part, the Attlee administration suspected some strikes as being motivated by pressure from the communists. This was so in the case of the ten-day strike by the workers of the North Thames Gas Board which led the government to arrest ten of the leaders, under Order 1305 and other legislation. They were sentenced to imprisonment for a month, although the sentence was later reduced to a fine.

The frustrations at the Attlee government's policies were mounting. The Labour left were disaffected, the trade unions were frustrated at wage controls, there were financial problems and the cost of Britain's involvement in the Korean War was rising rapidly. Although the 1950 general election returned Labour to office with 315 seats, compared with 393 in 1945, this was a much reduced majority of five which reflected Labour's problems. Faced with further problems, and dissension, including the resignation of Nye Bevan, Attlee called a further general election for October 1951. Though the Labour Party remained the most popular political party, with 48.8 per cent of the vote compared to the Conservative Party's 48 per cent, it captured only 295 seats compared to the 302 of the Conservatives. Labour's political high point had come to an end.

CONCLUSION

The Attlee Labour government faced many problems by the beginning of the 1950s. It was blighted by financial difficulties, challenged by the Labour left, unhappy with its dependency and association with the United States, and faced with serious challenges from the trade-union movement by the end of the 1940s. Nevertheless, it had introduced a modern welfare state, which went well beyond the social blueprint laid down by the Beveridge Report of 1942, and had created the National Health Service. It had also taken over some essential industries and services into public ownership. Indeed, the successes of the Labour government of 1945 to 1950 should be recognized. It offered the most effective evidence of what could be achieved by a democratic socialist administration. It brought about a change in direction for the British nation and moved government towards a more humanitarian concern for its people – committing it to the maintenance of full employment by Keynesian expansionism and state intervention – in sharp contrast to the sentiments that followed the First World War. These achievements were considerable and formed the basis of the policies of successive governments, at least until 1979. The Labour Party's disappointing electoral performances in the 1950 and 1951 general elections thus belie its immense social and political achievements.

CHAPTER SIX

Crisis in the Labour Party,
1951–79

Despite winning 48.8 per cent of the vote at the general election in 1951, Labour returned only 295 MPs to Parliament, 7 fewer than the Conservatives who won only 48.0 per cent of the vote. Although this defeat was a product of the British first-past-the-post system it did anticipate a protracted period of decline for the Labour Party. Indeed, Labour was out of office between 1951 and 1964, enjoyed a six-year period of power between 1964 and 1970, and was out of office again until the Wilson and Callaghan governments of 1974 to 1979. In other words, the Labour Party enjoyed office for only eleven years out of twenty-eight years and its star waned even further after 1979, when it was driven out of office for another eighteen years. It is, therefore, not surprising that many political commentators and historians have asked – why did Labour decline? By the 1980s and 1990s, even the Party faithfuls were asking the same question and becoming pessimistic about the likelihood of Labour ever winning office again.

Many explanations have been offered for Labour's decline. They range from the suggestion that Labour was not left-wing enough, failing to extend public ownership much beyond what it was in 1951, to the suggestion that Labour was too socialist for the British electorate. Undoubtedly, however, whatever the speculative analysis of historians, it has to be admitted that Labour's political decline had much to do with its political divisions in the 1950s, the changing nature of British society and the rising level of industrial conflict, which was also closely associated with the trade-union dominated Labour Party. Indeed, the 'winter of discontent' of 1978/9 played its part in convincing the electorate that the Labour Party was unfit to govern.[1]

BEVANISM *V* GAITSKELLISM

For some Labour critics the crucial period for Labour was the early 1950s when there was conflict between the Labour left and the Party leadership on the one hand, and between the Party leadership and the trade-union dominated Party on the other. In essence, this conflict was between the Labour left, or Bevanites, who wanted more socialism, the Gaitskellites, who wanted to abandon public ownership as the defining policy of socialism, and the Labour right and trade unions, who, despite their opposition to the Labour left, wished to retain public ownership, Clause Four, as their commitment to socialism. It is fair to suggest, then, that the Party was in more than its usual state of disarray.

The Bevanites, as a group, emerged from the Keep Left Group, discussed in detail in the previous chapter. Impetus was given to Keep Left by the defection of Aneurin Bevan and Harold Wilson from Attlee's government in April 1951 and by the fact that Michael Foot and Jennie Lee, editors of the left-wing paper *Tribune*, published *One Way Only*, with an introduction from Aneurin Bevan, demanding a reduction in defence expenditure and the stabilization of the cost of living.

The Bevanites numbered about thirty-two members in October 1951 but may have increased to as many as fifty-seven by the mid-1950s. Given that the May 1955 general election returned 277 Labour MPs, it would appear that the Bevanite section of the Party represented about 20 per cent of the Parliamentary Labour Party. It could not, therefore, be easily ignored by the Party leadership. Indeed, there were many key Labour figures within this grouping. Apart from Bevan, who later split away from the Bevanites, Barbara Castle, Tom Driberg, Ian Mikardo, Fenner Brockway, Jennie Lee and Richard Crossman were Bevanites.

As Richard Crossman made clear in his diaries, the Bevanites met frequently in the wake of the Labour government's defeat of 1951 and, in their early meetings, considered the appeal of Fenner Brockway and Jennie Lee to widen their influence.[2] They achieved this desire. At the 1952 Labour Party Conference the Bevanites managed to pass a resolution committing the Party to draw up a list of key industries to be taken into public ownership. Yet the General Council of the TUC and the National Executive Committee of the Labour Party submerged this demand by advocating further research into the matter.[3] The Bevanites were even less successful on the issues of British and German rearmament. In March 1952, fifty-seven Labour MPs defied the Labour Whips and voted against the Conservative government motion demanding reapproval for the rearmament programme in Britain. These Bevanites carried their views at the 1953 Labour Party Conference, when German rearmament was opposed. Nevertheless, the National Executive

Committee of the Party and the Parliamentary Labour Party felt confident enough to ignore the reservations of the Bevanites and to support the case for German rearmament in 1954. The Bevanite influence was further diminished by the fact that Bevan was a member of Labour's Shadow Cabinet between 1952 and 1954, and thus subject to collective responsibility towards the policies of the Party which prevented him too obviously leading the left opposition within the Labour Party. In addition, the Party reimposed its Standing Orders, suspended in 1945, which prevented Labour MPs defying the Party Whips except where they could invoke a narrowly defined 'conscience clause'.

Bevanism was nipped in the bud, even though Bevan gave up his seat on Labour's National Executive Committee in order to fight Hugh Gaitskell for the Treasurership of the Party. After his expected defeat he turned to organizing the rank-and-file trade unionists and was threatened with possible expulsion from the Labour Party in February and March 1955 for his action of defying the decision of the PLP to support manufacture of the hydrogen bomb. According to Richard Crossman there was little real possibility of Bevan being expelled, for Attlee, who was about to retire as the Party Leader, was too intent upon keeping the Labour Party united.[4] However, this was not the impression given in Hugh Gaitskell's diaries, where it is clear that he was discussing the possibility of making Bevan's expulsion a possible resignation issue.[5] In the end, although the Parliamentary Labour Party withdrew the Whip from Bevan, the NEC avoided expelling him from the Labour Party by one vote.[6]

Bevan soon became a spent force as the representative of the Labour left against the Party machine. Following Labour's unsuccessful performance in the 1955 general election, and the retirement of Attlee, he was decisively defeated by Hugh Gaitskell, the former Chancellor of the Exchequer, in the Labour leadership contest of December 1955. With his leadership hopes dashed, he soon became reconciled to working within the Party, becoming its Treasurer in October 1956 and returning to the Shadow Cabinet as Shadow Foreign Secretary, in November 1956. Bevan effectively divested himself of the title 'Leader of the Left' at the 1957 Labour Party conference by attacking the idea of unilateral disarmament, claiming to be unwilling to send a British foreign secretary 'naked into the conference chamber'. This action was a devastating shock to those who trusted in Bevan's support for unilateralism. One Bevanite reflected that it was an 'utter repudiation of everything for which Nye stood for three days before'.[7] Indeed, the 1957 Labour Party Conference as a whole saw the rapid demise of the left's influence within the Party and Crossman reflected that it was a complete victory for Gaitskell: 'After three years he has got his own interpretation of nationalization through without conceding an inch to his opponents and . . . he has maintained his position in nuclear weapons without conceding an inch in the Parliamentary Party.'[8] The Bevanites had proved no match for the revisionist Gaitskell.

Hugh Gaitskell and the Gaitskellites were able to dominate the Labour Party throughout the 1950s, though they could never remove Clause Four from the Labour Party Constitution. Gaitskell emerged from a wealthy middle-class background, was educated at Winchester and New College, Oxford, where he was taught by the socialist theorist G.D.H. Cole. Having become Labour MP for South Leeds in 1945, a seat which he held until his death in 1963, he was Minister of Fuel and Power between 1947 and 1950, Minister of State and Economic Affairs in 1950, and Chancellor of the Exchequer from 1950 to 1951. Once elected to replace Attlee, as Labour Leader, in 1955 he was determined to change the direction of some of Labour's socialist policies, most obviously its commitment to Clause Four, which he believed was unpopular with the British public and the cause of Labour's general election defeat in 1955. His views on this, and on the need for multilateral rather than unilateral disarmament, denoted him to be a 'revisionist' within the Labour Party – the leader of the 'Gaitskellite' revisionists.

The Gaitskellites were a loose grouping of politicians who hovered around Gaitskell, and included Anthony Crosland MP, John Strachey MP, and Dr Rita Hinden, who was very largely responsible for editing *Socialist Commentary*, a periodical of right-wing Labour opinion which was founded in 1942. The links between the various strands of this grouping were forged by Gaitskell, who was Treasurer of the friends of *Socialist Commentary* between 1953 and 1955. Through his friends in the trade-union movement, he was able to secure considerable financial support for that journal.

Anthony Crosland was the most important of the Gaitskellites and, like Gaitskell, had a middle-class background and an Oxford education. Although an Oxford don, he was returned to Parliament for South Gloucestershire in 1950, lost his seat in 1955 but returned as MP for Grimsby in 1959, holding the seat until his death in 1977. Obviously closely associated with Gaitskell in the mid-1950s his ideas gave rise to the term 'Croslandism', which was to reflect his particular brand of Gaitskellite 'revisionism'.[9]

At this particular juncture, there was a large range of opinion within the wider Labour movement. The Bevanites wanted more overtly socialist policies to be pursued by the Labour Party, and certainly more public ownership. The Communist Party of Great Britain was seeking to work within the parliamentary system, advocating its policy *The British Road to Socialism*, in which it accepted that socialism could be developed within Britain through the formation of a People's government which would introduce socialist legislation. The problem it faced was that it was still too closely associated with the policies of the Soviet Union and its intervention in Hungary in October and November 1956 which seemed to contradict its newly proclaimed acceptance of the British parliamentary and democratic tradition.

The views of the Gaitskellites were far more coherent than those of the Bevanites. On foreign policy, they expressed concern about the scale of rearmament in Britain, German rearmament and the development of nuclear weapons, but on the whole approved of these actions and adopted a multilateral attitude to nuclear disarmament. On domestic issues their views tended to stem from the assumption that capitalism had been fundamentally changed as a result of the successes of the Attlee governments. Gaitskell simply accepted that nationalization was no longer vital to socialism, since the controls of government and Keynesian interventionism permitted capitalism to be controlled and since he saw nationalization as the means to an end, and not the end in itself.[10] Anthony Crosland, the real intellect behind the Gaitskellite revisionists, was even more emphatic upon such points. His article in the *New Fabian Essays* (1952) maintained that the power which property owners had wielded had been dissipated due to the fact that industry was now run by professional managers and civil servants. This meant that there was no urgent need to nationalize industry. In addition, the proliferation of social services meant that the redistribution of income through direct taxation was no longer essential.[11]

Crosland's views were developed further in his book *The Future of Socialism* (1956), the most forceful attempt to reinterpret the meaning of socialism in the light of the changes that had taken place since 1945. He argued that the growth of democratic pressures and the rapid expansion of the economy had invalidated the Marxist theory of the inevitable collapse of capitalism for there was now full employment, a radical welfare programme and a strong trade-union movement. He also accepted that nationalization was no longer vitally important and that in future socialism must turn to the development of socialist ideals, a moral or ethical way of life, for the Labour Party could not simply defend the programme that it had introduced between 1945 and 1951.

These revisionist ideas became more important when Gaitskell became Labour Party Leader in December 1955, though they had won some support in the early 1950s. By 1953 Labour had more or less dropped the idea of drawing up a shopping list of industries to be nationalized in favour of further research and planning. In 1957 the revisionist views were reaching their zenith with the publication, and acceptance by the Labour Conference, of *Industry and Society: Labour's Policy on Future Public Ownership*, a document which played down the need for further public ownership and suggested that alternative types of common ownership were possible.

Many now felt that Labour had to offer itself as a moderate and respectable party, free from class bias. According to Gaitskell, the Labour Party needed to focus upon the needs of a working class which was being imbued with middle-class values. For that reason it had to play down its socialism. Gaitskell thus launched his attack upon old shibboleths at the Blackpool Conference in 1959.

Yet Gaitskell's revisionism could only go as far as the dominant trade unions would allow. On most matters the major trade unions accepted the National Executive Committee of the Labour Party's policies but, in 1959 and 1960, they rejected Gaitskell's famous attempt to remove Clause Four from the Party Constitution (see Introduction and Chapter Two).

Gaitskell, motivated by Labour's defeat at the general election of 1959, reflected that the Labour Party had performed well in the campaign but had still lost the election by more than 100 seats. He reasoned that this must be the result of the changing social and economic composition of the electorate and presented this view to the Blackpool conference in 1959:

> We may be far from the frontier of this kind of giant State monopoly . . . [but] I cannot agree that we have reached the frontier of public ownership as a whole.
>
> At the same time I disagree with the other extreme view that public ownership is the be all and end all, the ultimate first principle and aim of socialism.[12]

The goal to be achieved was not 100 per cent state ownership but the creation of a society in which socialist ideals could be realized. However, Gaitskell's speech was criticized by both the Labour left and the Labour right. Richard Crossman repeated the left's hostility towards the revisionist ideas of Gaitskell and Frank Cousin, leader of the Transport and General Workers' Union, and rejected the attempt to remove Clause Four.

At the 1960 Party Conference matters got worse when a motion supporting unilateral disarmament was passed by 3.3 million votes to 2.9 million, provoking Gaitskell to declare that he would 'fight and fight again' to save the Party. However, at the Party Conference, in October 1961, Gaitskell got this decision overturned by 4.5 million votes to 1.7 million. However, he was unable to remove Clause Four from the Labour Constitution and a demand for wider public ownership was accepted at the Conference by 3.7 million to 2.4 million votes.

Gaitskell was never likely to be able to get the Labour Party to remove Clause Four and this was recognized when Morgan Phillips, the newly titled General Secretary of the Party (the title changed from Secretary to General Secretary in 1959), issued *Labour in the Sixties*, which was presented and accepted at the 1960 Party Conference. This programme statement made no attempt to reject Clause Four but argued a clear Gaitskellite line throughout:

In the 1960s Socialism will win more support only when it is recognized that it offers a better way and that it can make a unique contribution to solving the problems of the scientific age. Brute poverty and unemployment can happily, no longer be expected to act as the recruiting sergeants of the Labour movement . . .

In recent years they (the opposition) have tried to present us as an old, backward-looking party – restrictive and bureaucratic when in office, divided and quarrelling when in opposition. And we should frankly face the fact that we have sometimes given them, in our own conduct, enough evidence to make such a charge stick.[13]

The attempt to revitalize the Party remained the preoccupation of Gaitskell and his supporters. The demand was for a young, active and united party that would face up to the changes in British society.

The antagonisms between the Bevanites and the Gaitskellites had arisen out of the different perceptions of the way in which the Labour

Party could recapture power. The Bevanites had opposed what they perceived to be the retreat from socialism, convinced that in some way the development of socialist ideas and policies, firmly supported by the Party, would win back Labour's lost votes. This flatly contradicted the views of the Gaitskellites who were adamant that the objective conditions of British society had changed and that Labour had to see beyond Clause Four and the support of the old working class. The problem is that neither strand offered any positive policies for the future other than the defence or the abandonment of Clause Four. In the hands of the Labour Party, socialism appeared to be either a static or waning philosophy – there was little sign of advance. There was certainly little evidence that the Labour Party was responding to some of the social changes that were becoming evident in the 1950s and 1960s.

British society was, indeed, changing rapidly. In 1950 the white-collar workers represented about 30 per cent of the British workforce; by 1979 the proportion had risen to about 52 per cent. Over the same period the proportion of manual workers fell from 64.2 per cent to about 45 per cent. As a result, the traditional occupational bastions of Labour Party support have declined. In mining and quarrying, for instance, employment has fallen from 880,000 in 1948 to 629,000 in 1965 and, more recently, to 250,000 in 1984 and less than 30,000 by the end of the 1990s. The National Union of Mineworkers has, as a result, shrunk dramatically. By the same token, the expansion of the white-collar workers has seen the rapid growth of trade-union membership. The Association of Scientific, Technical and Managerial Staffs rose from 123,000 members in 1970 to 427,500 in 1982.

Some of this growth in the service and white-collar sector has been due to the rise in female employment. The female participation ratio rose from 34.7 per cent in 1951 to 42.7 per cent in 1971 and 47.4 per cent in 1977. More than one-third of all women were employed in part-time work by the end of the 1970s and a large number were employed in the low-paid clerical sector and service industries. Imposed upon a changing structure of employment has been a general increase in real incomes, which rose by a quarter in the 1950s alone, and the manifestations of greater wealth – the rising demand for consumer items and the strong move towards home ownership which meant that 53 per cent of British families were home owners in 1976.

Such changes and signs of affluence were not always recognized by the Labour Party, even though Tony Crosland and Hugh Gaitskell were attempting to force the Labour Party to diversify its style of socialism and recognize the need to attract both middle-class and working-class support. Clause Four was obviously of questionable value in attracting middle-class support and the Labour Party was rather negligent in developing its policies to attract women voters.

As a result the Labour Party made little impact in the 1955 and 1959 general elections. In 1955, with Attlee as Leader, Labour found both its proportion of the electorate and number of MPs decline and the situation, with Hugh Gaitskell as Labour Leader, had worsened in the 1959 general election. Indeed, the number of Labour MPs had declined from 295 in 1951 to 277 in 1955 and 258 in 1959 (see Appendices 3 and 4). The divisions within the Labour Party, and confusion over policy, seem to have worked to undermine the confidence in the Party – so much so that Labour's third general election defeat led Mark Abrams, Richard Rose and Rita Hinden to analyse the 1959 general election defeat in the pamphlet *Must Labour Lose?*[14] They maintained that the answer was probably yes, for three main reasons. Firstly, they noted the contraction of heavy industry which meant a reduction in the size of the traditional working class and the comparative expansion of the middle class and the middle-income group. Secondly, they suggested that social changes in society meant that middle-class values were expanding and that this increased consumerism at the expense of socialism. Thirdly, in consequence, Clause Four was losing its political appeal. This was a ringing endorsement of the Gaitskell approach which the Labour Party proved reluctant to take. While the Bevanites were isolated and defeated the 'revisionists' or 'new thinkers' as they were sometimes called, were neutralized and found their main objective – the removal of Clause Four – defeated.

LABOUR'S REVIVAL IN THE 1960S

In 1960 it appeared that the Labour Party might be a spent political force. Hugh Gaitskell was trying, unsuccessfully, to give a 'revisionist' slant to an 'Old' Labour Party dominated by the trade unions who were unwilling to change. The temporary alliance between the Labour left and the Labour right, represented in the fact that Gaitskell, the Labour Leader, had acquired Aneurin Bevan as his Deputy Leader in 1959, was at an end following the death of Bevan in 1960. By 1961 the Labour Party seemed somewhat divided on the issue of the European Economic Community (EEC) or Common Market as well. In July 1961, Harold Macmillan had launched his bid for entry to the EEC and this presented problems for the Labour Party. Gaitskell felt that Macmillan's conditions for entry were going to undermine the position of the Commonwealth but was worried about the prospects of a further split within the Labour Party which might damage the prospects for victory – a split that would have been hot on the heels of the divisive defence/nuclear debate within the Party in 1960–1.

Possible British entry to the EEC raised the issue of Britain's relations with the rest of the world and cut across the Labour left and Labour right splits which had dominated the issues of Clause Four and defence. While Gaitskell and, indeed, the lately deceased Bevan, believed in the world role of Britain, to which the EEC was an irrelevance, some young members of the Party, most obviously Roy Jenkins, believed in the need to work more closely with the EEC. The Labour Party was likely to be split.

The problem for Gaitskell was to keep the Party together. It was believed that the majority of the Labour Party was opposed to membership of the EEC but this support came mainly from the trade-union forces and the left who had opposed the Gaitskellites on Clause Four and had advocated unilateral disarmament. Of the Gaitskellites, possibly three-quarters were actually pro-EEC.[15] Gaitskell, in order to maintain Party unity, and in order to express his own misgivings about Europe, stressed that protection must be given to British agriculture, and the interests of Britain's partners in the Commonwealth and the European Free Trade Association (EFTA was a free-trade area comprising several nations in western Europe who were not part of the EEC). He felt that Macmillan's bid for entry to the EEC would be at a cost to all these interests. In his powerful speech at the Labour Party's Brighton Conference in the autumn of 1962 Gaitskell added rational arguments to an emotional tone to reject the idea of joining the EEC and ending Britain's history as an independent state. In the nationalistic part to his speech he stated that:

> We must be clear about this: it does mean, if this is the idea, the end of Britain as an independent European state. I make no apology for repeating it. It means the end of a thousand years of history. You may say, 'Let it end', but my goodness, it is a decision that needs a little care and thought. And does it mean the end of the Commonwealth? How can one seriously suppose if the mother country, the centre of

the Commonwealth, is a province of Europe (which is what Federation means) it could continue to exist as the mother country of a series of independent nations? It is sheer nonsense.[16]

Gaitskell, at the end of his speech, outlined the possibility of entry if the conditions that he outlined – the safeguarding of the Commonwealth interests, the safeguarding of Britain's agricultural interests and the safeguarding of EFTA interests – could be met. In this way the Brighton Labour Party Conference was able to pass a non-committal motion on entry to the EEC and avoid a serious Party split until the moment that Macmillan's Conservative government negotiations faltered.

Gaitskell had maintained Party unity at a difficult time but there still seemed little prospect that Labour would significantly improve its immediate political fortunes. The transformation of this situation appears to have occurred when Harold Wilson, an old ally of Aneurin Bevan, became Leader of the Party, following the untimely death of Gaitskell in January 1963 at the age of 56. In succeeding to the leadership, Wilson defeated George Brown and James Callaghan, the later Labour Leader, in the process.

From the outset, Wilson decided that Labour could no longer sustain itself on the old rhetoric of social distribution but that it had to relate its policies to the need to achieve economic growth. For this reason he accepted the need to modernize the British economy. There was to be a National Plan for growth by which Labour would release the pent-up forces of 'white-hot' technology. The Labour Party Conference of 1963 accepted this proposal and the trade unions agreed they would also accept a comprehensive incomes policy.

Yet Party programmes, such as *Labour in the Sixties* and its successor, *Signposts for the Sixties*, anticipated Wilson's later initiatives. The latter had begun by announcing that 'We live in a scientific revolution' and followed this up by suggesting that Britain needed to harness the forces of science for the community, to supervise the balanced growth of the economy and to ensure the fair distribution of wealth.[17] The document was besotted with the belief that the scientific revolution would make everything possible. Labour's 1964 manifesto had thus called for state-led modernization.

Yet Labour's victory in the general election of 1964 did not permit the transformation which Wilson would have liked. His majority of four was too narrow to achieve the initiatives[18] which he had envisaged and, indeed, the new Labour government was faced with an economic crisis which forced it to introduce a deflationary package in 1965. Nevertheless, Labour's victory restored much confidence to a Party which had been so recently contemplating the prospect of never gaining office again. The tremendous victory which the Labour Party gained in the 1966 general election when, with 364 MPs, it secured an overall majority of 98, confirmed it in its rising confidence that it was the Party of power and government. It had secured for itself a sense of balance and authority. Yet this moment of confidence and euphoria was fleeting. By the end of the 1960s the mood had gone. What went wrong?

The economic problems of the late 1960s and the inability of the Wilson government of 1966 to 1970, to deal with the trade unions confirmed to many voters that Labour had difficulty in running the economy effectively. Indeed, Wilson recognized this problem himself and in 1966 and 1967 decided that a fresh application for membership of the European Economic Community was in order. The French vetoed this move in May 1967 at a moment when relations between the government and the trade unions was declining further.

Labour had secured trade-union support for an incomes policy in 1963, before it came to power, and had set up a National Board for Prices and Incomes in 1965. However, these policies never worked effectively. Strikes, particularly the seamen's strike of May 1966, the wage freeze of 1966 and the devaluation of the pound in 1967, destroyed the trust between the Labour government and the trade unions. Indeed, the trade unions were in open revolt against the Labour government in 1969 when, in the wake of the Royal Commission on Trade Unions and Employers' Organizations (the Donovan Commission), the Labour government published *In Place of Strife*, a White Paper on industrial relations.

Although *In Place of Strife* offered a number of advantages, most notably protection from 'unfair dismissal' for their members, trade unions were sensitive to the proposal that they would be registered and that their right to work would be impaired. It had suggested that the government might be empowered to settle inter-union disputes, that in the case of unofficial strikes the Secretary of State would have the power to issue an order to impose a 'conciliation pause' of twenty-eight days, and have the right to order secret ballots for official strikes which were considered to 'involve a serious threat to the economy or public interest'.[19] The whole package suggested that trade unions were no longer to be free to conduct industrial relations on the voluntary basis which they had enjoyed for almost a century in peacetime Britain. In consequence, the TUC held a special conference, mobilized its opposition to the White Paper, and even forced the National Executive Committee of the Labour Party to vote against its acceptance. The White Paper had to be withdrawn; the Labour government was humbled by the trade unions.

In its desire to make British industry more efficient the government had tackled an issue on which it could only lose. If it took action against strikes then it threatened the link between the working class, the trade unions and the Party which had always been vital to Labour's growth. If, on the other hand, it did not face up to the problem of strikes then, to the electorate at large, it demonstrated its incapacity to govern and its unwillingness to move beyond sectional interests. Was Labour to be the party of the unions or the party of the nation? The events surrounding the publication of *In Place of Strife* suggested that it might be neither. The Labour government's trade-union support certainly began to dip at this point and its credibility as a party of government was greatly diminished as wages rose sharply to the rate of 13 per cent per annum. In this climate, Labour lost the 1970 general election to Edward Heath's Conservative Party. A Labour majority of ninety-six was thus turned into a Conservative majority of thirty in June 1970. The fragility of Labour's hopes and aspirations in the 1960s had been exposed by its failure to achieve significant economic growth and its failure to deal effectively with the trade unions.

THE 1970S, A DECADE OF FURTHER DISILLUSION

Despite its setback, with 288 MPs Labour was still a powerful force in the House of Commons, and the Heath government faced serious industrial difficulties following its attempt to impose industrial discipline. Its conflicts with the miners in 1972/3 and 1974 were events that opened it up to criticism and undoubtedly led to its defeat in the general election of February 1974. Indeed, the Labour Party was eventually returned by the electorate to deal with these problems.

As a backcloth to the industrial problems of the Heath government, and Labour's response to them, there was also the issue of the European Economic Community. Edward Heath's Conservative government signed the Treaty of Accession in 1972 and Britain joined the EEC in 1973. Although the Labour Party and the Parliamentary Labour Party were opposed to membership of the EEC there were sixty-nine Labour MPs, led by Roy Jenkins, who had been prepared to vote in favour of membership when it came to a parliamentary vote in October 1971. The issue was clearly deeply divisive.

Harold Wilson, still Labour Leader, attempted to deal with both the EEC and Labour's economic policies in 1973. At the 1973 Blackpool Conference, the Labour Party rejected a motion for the nationalization of 250 major monopolies, voted to continue to boycott the EEC institutions until membership was confirmed by a referendum or general election, and adopted *Labour's Programme, 1973*, calling for 'a fundamental and irreversible shift in the balance of power and wealth in favour of working people. It thus called for an extension of public ownership, even though right-wingers such as Tony Crosland had argued that there was no link between public ownership and equality. Nevertheless, while it is possible that these policies may have made Labour attractive to the electorate it was the problem of the industrial relations of the Heath government that brought it to power. However, victory for Labour was something of a poisoned chalice as they had inherited a high level of inflation and a wage policy which triggered wage increases as inflation rose further, thus potentially spawning further inflation.

Clearly, the Labour Party had been returned to power to deal more constructively with industrial relations following the introduction of the Industrial Relations Act of 1971, with its measures for a sixty-day 'cooling-off' period and for pre-strike ballots. Yet the electorate's judgement had been a negative one, for the Party was returned as a minority government faced with a combined opposition majority against it of thirty-three. Even the October 1974 general election, which gave Labour an overall majority of three, was hardly evidence of the great confidence of the British electorate in the Labour Party. Indeed, from 1977, as parliamentary by-election defeats took their toll, the Labour government, by now under James Callaghan who had replaced Wilson in 1976, was forced to make a political arrangement with the Liberal Party in order to retain power. Weak Labour governments were thus faced with the problems of dealing more effectively with the pressing problems of curbing trade-union power, improving industrial relations, and raising the level of economic growth.

The damaging impression that Labour could not deal with the trade unions remained a serious threat to its political future, and a constant worry for Party Leaders. Although an inside account of the events is not available until 2004 to 2009, because of the thirty-year restriction on government records, the records of the Trades Union Congress and the published diaries and books of those ministers who were close to the events provide us with a clear, if partial, indication of the pattern of events surrounding the emergence and failure of the 'Social Contract', the arrangement between the Labour government and the trade unions to control wage demands in return for the redistribution of income and resources.

At the Labour Party Conference in 1971, when Labour was in opposition, Harold Wilson appealed to the unions 'to accept the economic realities and understand the political responsibilities we face in Government'.[20] Trade-union leaders were quick to respond and even the normally cautious Hugh Scanlon of the Amalgamated Union of Engineering Workers acknowledged the need for unity. 'There had been too much blood letting, too much acrimony, too much disillusionment – and trade unions were not blameless in this – with all the harmful effects that accrued in June 1970, for these mistakes ever to be repeated again'.

The Labour Party and the TUC moved towards rapprochement, and *Labour's Programme*, adopted at the Party Conference at Blackpool in 1973, recognized the need to establish a balance between full employment, economic growth, a healthy balance of payments and moderate levels of inflation. To make the whole process work effectively, trade unions had to accept a voluntary incomes policy while government would redistribute income and resources on an annual basis. The Labour Party programme recognized the need for a far-reaching social contract between workers and government.

Such accord was short-lived once the Labour government came to office in 1974, largely because Labour faced the dilemma of economic stagnation at a time when it was offering a programme of increased government spending to win trade-union support in obtaining voluntary wage restraint. At first it appeared that Wilson's government, formed in February 1974, was attempting to make the Social Contract work. The compulsory wage restraints, imposed by Heath's government, were jettisoned in July 1974, a new Ministry of Prices, Consumer Protection and Fair Trading was established, and food subsidies introduced in Denis Healey's first budget. The Industrial Relations Act of 1971 was also repealed. As Barbara Castle suggested, in her published diaries, the Cabinet and Wilson were intent upon playing straight down the line of agreed Party policy, at least until the spring of 1975, when inflationary pressures became too great.[21] Nevertheless, Barbara Castle, the architect of *In Place of Strife*, perceived that there might be penalties to pay in adopting a voluntary policy at a time of balance of payments difficulties. She was right. Faced with serious financial difficulties the Labour government imposed a £6 per week wage rise limit, with a zero increase for those earning above £8,500 per annum. This was the beginning of the end for the Social Contract.

The fact is that the Wilson government failed to achieve the economic growth it aimed for, against a background of rising unemployment and inflation. It also abandoned its promised increased public control over private industry and its commitment to extending social welfare provisions, although ailing firms such as British Leyland and British Aerospace were taken into public ownership. Indeed, although government minister Shirley Williams, worried that Tony Benn, Labour's Secretary of State for Industry, 'had alarmed industrialists' because 'We must carry industrialists with us, they are on the edge of total non-cooperation', there had been no need for her to worry.[22] Benn was replaced in his role in 1975.

Unemployment rose from 678,000 to 1,129,000 during the course of 1975 and the Labour government panicked and introduced an austerity budget which transferred resources from the private to the public sector and reduced public spending planned for 1977–8 by £900 million, at the expense of about 20,000 jobs. This was followed by the £6 per week wage increase limit, already mentioned, in July 1975. The Labour government had returned to an old-style incomes policy and matters grew worse when Denis Healey, the Chancellor of the Exchequer, was forced to approach the International Monetary Fund to secure a massive loan. When the deal was struck in December 1975, the Labour government was faced with the necessity of pruning government expenditure by another £2,500 million in order to secure a loan of £3,000 million – which created immense tensions and rival responses within the Labour Cabinet.[23] The government was thus forced to abandon any idea it had of expanding public control over industry.

Nevertheless, Labour did resolve the issue of the European Economic Community for its members. It had agreed, as part of its general election manifesto, to seek new terms for Britain's membership and to put these to the British nation in a referendum. As a result of negotiations with the EEC the Labour government recommended acceptance of the new terms in a referendum on British membership in June 1975. Wilson took the unusual action of allowing his ministers to campaign for or against these new terms and some anti-marketeers, such as Tony Benn, participated in the 'Britain out' campaign while Roy Jenkins led the pro-Common Market campaign. Eventually, by more than a 2:1 majority, the electorate voted in favour of Britain staying within Europe and accepting the new terms. The British electorate had decided and Party unity was maintained.

It was nine months after the referendum and at the height of trade-union frustration at the Labour government's failure to deliver its part of the Social Contract, that in March 1976, Harold Wilson abruptly announced his intention to retire, fulfilling his previous, but largely ignored, statement that he would retire when he reached sixty. He had only just narrowly survived a vote of 'no confidence' and may have taken this as a sign that now was the time to go.

The Party leadership contest in April pitted six of Labour's leading political figures against each other and, at the third ballot, returned James Callaghan as Party Leader, and thus Prime Minister, ahead of Michael Foot. Callaghan's new administration had little more success than Wilson's previous one, and soon after becoming Prime Minister he announced that there had to be a new economic realism about Labour. At the Labour Party Conference of 1976 he made a seminal speech in which he said:

> We used to think that you could spend your way out of recession and increase employment by cutting taxes and boosting Government spending. I will tell you with candour that that option no longer exists, and that insofar as it ever did exist, it only worked on each occasion since the war by injecting a bigger dose of inflation into the economy, followed by a higher level of unemployment as the next step.[24]

The Labour Party and Britain had changed economic course. The commitment to expanding out of slump to tackle unemployment, the Keynesian solution, was at an end. This soon became apparent in Labour's economic policies.

Denis Healey's April 1977 Budget Stage 1 provided £1,300 million in tax reductions provided that the TUC accepted the continuation of wage restraint and, in May 1977, Stage 2 of the government's anti-inflationary wages policy set pay-rise limits of £2.50 minimum and £4.00 maximum per week. The TUC agreed to hold a special conference to discuss the matter but the further government announcement of a £1,000 million spending reduction for 1977–8 undermined any prospect of compromise with the TUC. By this time the Labour government was visibly rocking. Its overall majority of three, achieved on 3 October 1974, was gone and, in March 1977, it was only saved from a Conservative censure motion by Liberal Party support, following the negotiation of a Liberal-Labour pact.

Inevitably, industrial relations grew worse. In July 1977 Stage 3 of the government's incomes policy provided a 10 per cent limit on wage rises and Denis Healey, the Chancellor of the Exchequer, threatened to financially penalize employers who broke that limit. Thus it became apparent that the government was not going to redistribute income and resources, its part of the 'Social Contract' arrangement. By November 1977 there was a direct threat to the new wage limit when the firefighters began a strike for a 30 per cent pay increase in breach of the government's incomes policy. By the autumn of 1978 matters were reaching crisis proportions. The Labour Party Conference, dominated by trade-union votes, rejected the government's new 5 per cent pay guideline in October and, in November, the TUC General Council also rejected the new guidelines. The TUC had now formally decided to return to free collective bargaining and rejected totally any further wage restraint.[25] In a climate of rising unemployment and reduced public expenditure, industrial unrest rocketed in the autumn of 1978 and in early 1979 about 150,000 employees were laid off as a result of the road haulage strike. This 'winter of discontent' put paid to any hopes that Labour had of winning the 1979 general election. Instead, in May 1979 Labour gained a mere 39.9 per cent of the vote, its lowest percentage since 1931, and won only 269 seats.

In asking why the Labour Party/government had done so badly between 1974 and 1979 it is clear that much of the failure was to do with industrial relations. That is not to say that the Labour government did not have some successes and other major problems to face. There were problems with Northern Ireland, and the suspension of the Northern Ireland Assembly in 1974. Britain's entry to the EEC, in January 1973, which had been opposed by a 5:1 majority at the Labour Party Conference in October 1971, was settled effectively by a more than 2:1 majority referendum in favour of remaining a member of the EEC in June 1975. A potentially divisive issue within the Labour Party was thus settled by the electorate. Nevertheless, there remained the economic problems of the nation and the inability of the government to deal with them effectively.

It may be futile to examine whether more or less radical programmes, or more public ownership, would have retained or increased the political appeal of Labour, for the primary obstacle to the mobilization of political support for Labour was the contrast between its promise and achievement in office. This may help to explain the declining support for nationalization as a policy which, in any case, has not substantially altered the position of the worker. Perhaps the most serious failure, though, was the seemingly cynical abandonment of the 1974 programme soon after the Labour Party had taken office, when its rapid retreat into conventional and conservative economic and social programmes revealed its ultimate political bankruptcy. The heady optimism of the early 1970s, that the Labour Party in power could use its close relationship with the trade-union movement and its declared intention to use state intervention to create a more equal society in which employment was secure and economic growth sustained, had gone by 1979, if not earlier. The *Guardian* had detected that the government was having difficulty in financing the growing social expenditure, noting that 'popular expectations about improvements in welfare programmes and public service have not been matched by any willingness to give up improvements in living standards in favour of these programmes'.[26] The issue was quite clear: the Labour government could not sustain its welfare programme without increasing taxation, and thus the cost of living, and threatening the very trade-union members whose voluntary agreement to limit wage increases was vital if industrial costs were to be kept down and if confidence in the pound was to be maintained. In the end, the poor financial position of the government, a weak pound, and slow industrial growth forced the abandonment of the voluntary incomes policy and necessitated cutbacks in social and welfare measures and the redistribution of wealth in Britain. These were actions which the Labour Party's most militant erstwhile trade-union supporters found difficult to accept.

The Labour governments of the 1960s and 1970s failed to encourage rapid economic growth, did not deliver their promises and found themselves embroiled in conflict with the unions. Out of these failures emerged support for the views of the New Right – whose policies of cutting state expenditure, shaking out surplus labour, and of unleashing the traditional forces of liberal capitalism did not seem out of tune with the actions of the 1970s Wilson and Callaghan governments, which had presided over welfare cuts and rising unemployment. The unthinkable had happened. The welfare state was no longer sacrosanct.

CONCLUSION

Between 1951 and 1979 the Labour Party underwent a major transformation in its position and fortunes. The decline in traditional heavy industry, and the overall contraction of the manufacturing industries, led to a reduction in Labour's traditional working-class support. In addition, there was a loosening of the ties between the trade unions and the Labour Party, occasioned by the industrial conflict of the late 1960s and the late 1970s. The economic and political failures of the Wilson and Callaghan governments in the 1970s certainly engendered much frustration at the reformist policies of the Party and called into question whether or not economic growth could be sustained through Labour's policies and whether or not a fundamental change in direction was called for. All these factors diminished the Labour Party and raised doubts about the political consensus of welfare politics, upon which its postwar politics had been gained. Out of Labour's dismal record in office under Wilson and Callaghan had arisen increasing support for the New Right philosophy which sought to marginalize the politics of the welfare state.

Yet the most fundamental reasons for Labour's decline, underpinning most other factors, was the reluctance of the Labour Party to adapt to the changing nature of British society. The old shibboleths, based upon the trade-union objectives of a fairer treatment for the working class, were trotted out at successive general elections, despite the fact that the Labour Party was becoming an increasingly middle-class party in the House of Commons. Gaitskell and the revisionists saw the need to break the class image of the Party in the 1950s and urged it to offer policies which would attract support for all the social classes. This attempt, just like Bevan's campaign to place socialism at the front of Labour Party policies, foundered on the rock of trade unionism. The culmination of Labour's failure to recognize the need for change was the formation of the Social Democratic Party in 1981, which saw four Labour right-wingers – Shirley Williams, Roy Jenkins, Bill Rodgers and David Owen – form a party which offered policies geared to the needs of the lower middle-class and professional workers.

The problem that faced the Labour Party in the late 1970s and early 1980s was that it found itself thrust back to its trade-union and working-class base at a time when the base was contracting rapidly. Yet it faced the dilemma that it could not abandon that base without losing the financial resources upon which it depended. It is this problem which the leaders of the Labour Party were forced to address in the 1980s and 1990s. They had to reduce the dependence of the Labour Party on the trade unions and to attract broader political support. As a result they inched the Labour Party towards redefining its socialism and its attitude towards Clause Four.

CHAPTER SEVEN

Despair, Reconstruction and Revival

The Labour Party from Foot to Blair, 1979–94

Margaret Thatcher led the Conservative Party to an emphatic victory in the general election of 3 May 1979. The Conservatives won 339 seats, with 43.9 per cent of the vote, while Labour won a mere 269 seats with 36.9 per cent of the vote. After swinging strongly to the left under Michael Foot, and promoting further commitments to nationalization, Labour lost again, disastrously, in the June 1983 general election, winning a mere 209 seats and, at that time, looked likely to fall to minor party status alongside the Liberals and the Social Democrats. Rather memorably, MP Gerald Kaufmann described Labour's 1983 manifesto as 'the longest suicide note in history', nailed as it was to the issue of nationalization. Under Neil Kinnock, the new Leader from 1983, Labour's political position gradually improved as the Party drifted in a rightward direction in its attempt to abandon the policies of nationalization and unilateral disarmament, and Labour performed more effectively in the 1987 general election, winning 229 seats. By the 1992 general election Labour even looked electable when Neil Kinnock ran what appeared to be an effective and triumphalist election campaign. In the end, Labour gained only 271 seats and was broadly back to the position it had been at the time of the 1979 general election. Yet with only 34.4 per cent of the vote, less than in 1979, it is not surprising that many political pundits and Labour politicians were pessimistic about Labour's political future. The Labour Party seemed to be set fair for a future of permanent opposition.

Indeed, Anthony Heath, Roger Jewell, John Curtice and Bridget Taylor edited a book, *Labour's Last Chance? The 1992 Election and Beyond*, the title of which obviously echoed the *Must Labour Lose?* book of 1960.[1] In this new book, as much as the earlier one, the general answer was probably yes. Thus the pessimism of the 1960s had visited the Labour Party in the 1990s, born of frustration and failure. From the 1999 position, of Tony Blair's Labour government being in office, this might appear surprising but it is clear that much went wrong for the Labour Party in the 1980s and early 1990s and that it had failed to fully adjust to the fact that its traditional trade-union and working-class base was being undermined. Nor was it attracting sufficient of the growing skilled sections of British society or much support in the southern and south-eastern part of England to guarantee its future as a party of government. This was not from want of action but it is clear that, between 1979 and 1994, the Labour Party was still perceived by the electorate to be controlled by the trade unions, committed to nationalization, wedded to pacifism, and incapable of dealing with the nation's finances – even though that image was, by then, outdated.

1979–83: A DIVIDED PARTY

The four years between Labour's defeat at the general election in May 1979 and its subsequent defeat in June 1983 were its bleakest ones since the political defection of James Ramsay MacDonald in 1931. They saw the Party lose its right wing to the Social Democratic Party in 1981, deep divisions develop within the Party, and a failure of leadership. It seemed Labour was wrenched apart between the left and right wings, who were involved in the bitter internecine conflict which paved the way for the Party's disastrous performance in the 1983 election.

In the immediate wake of defeat, reform was afoot. At the Labour Party Conference in 1979 it was decided that every Labour MP had to seek re-selection from their constituency during the lifetime of each Parliament, and that the Party National Executive, not the Party leadership, should have the final say on the contents of the general election manifesto – denoting that the trade unions were exercising their influence. The Conference also decided that a Committee of Enquiry would be set up to investigate the Party's organization.

At this stage the trade unions still dominated the Party Conference through the block vote, much to the annoyance of the right-wing and middle-class section of the Party's MPs. Constituency parties did allow the influence of individual members to dominate and could now establish whether their MP ought to be reselected, and the Parliamentary Labour Party (of all MPs), still selected the Labour Leader. There was certainly pressure for both the powers and influence of trade unions and MPs to be limited and for the individual membership of the Party to be drawn more clearly into the decision-making process. Such reform was, however, subject to pressure from the vested interests and the varying views, and political positions, of those who wanted reform. There was going to be no easy route to change, especially given that some MPs wanted a reduction in trade-union influence while many trade unionists and MPs wanted to share in the selection of the Party Leader.

Above all, the problem was that the Party was increasingly divided between the right-wingers, including Shirley Williams and David Owen, who wanted to play down the public ownership/nationalization aspects of Labour's policies and to capture a wider and more middle-class vote and the left-wingers who felt that Labour's future success could only be achieved by a swing back to its traditional trade-union and working-class support. Was the Party to go to the right or the left? Essentially, at this point the Party went to the left, as it had been doing since the early 1970s, and this led to the defection, to the Social Democratic Party, of some of the leading right-wing Labour MPs in 1981.

The events that led to the defection of its right-wingers began in the 1970s. In 1973 a small number of rank-and-file Party members formed themselves into the Campaign for Labour Party Democracy (CLPD), and were joined by other groups such as the Labour Coordinating Committee (LCC) and Militant Tendency, a splinter group from the Trotskyite movement which was ultimately committed to violent revolutionary change. Collectively, these groups gained increasing influence within the trade unions in the two years after the 1979 general election. They drove forward with three demands: to give the Labour Party Conference alone, and not MPs, the power to choose the Party Leader, to fix a programme of policies which Labour would be forced to follow once in power, and to demand that Labour MPs should face mandatory reselection by their constituency Labour Party during the lifetime of each Parliament. The aim was that such measures would reduce the power and influence of the right within the Party, allowing activists in the constituencies to influence decisions more effectively.

As already indicated, the mandatory reselection of sitting MPs in the life of each Parliament was accepted at the Labour Party Conference in 1979, along with a decision to give the left-wing dominated National Executive Committee of the Labour Party control over the general election manifesto. The latter decision was in fact reversed at the Labour Party Conference in 1980. Yet the crucial issue, for both the Labour left and the Labour right was the procedure for electing the Party Leader.

A week before the 1979 Party Conference the NEC had set up a Committee of Enquiry to recommend constitutional changes to the 1980 Conference. Denis Healey, and others, opposed this committee on the grounds that it was unrepresentative of the Party as a whole – the NEC sending seven left-wingers to the committee, the trade unions a balanced group of five and the Labour MPs only two members, James Callaghan and Michael Foot. Denis Healey's opposition was ignored and the Committee of Enquiry set out to create a new electoral college for the election of the Party Leader at the 1980 Party Conference.[2]

The Committee of Enquiry held its final meeting at Bishop's Stortford, and recommended that 50 per cent of the electoral college vote would be held by Labour MPs, 25 per cent by trade unions, 20 per cent by constituency parties and 5 per cent by other bodies such as the Fabian Society. This college was to choose the Party Leader and to have the final say on the Party's manifesto.

The suggested electoral arrangement was attacked by both the Labour left and the Labour right: the left fearing that it would keep power in the hands of the right-wing MPs, while the right felt that the proposal would destroy the traditional independence of Labour MPs. Not surprisingly the following meeting of the Shadow Cabinet saw David Owen and Bill Rodgers attack James Callaghan for betraying the Parliamentary Labour Party. Callaghan responded by attacking them for supporting Roy Jenkins's recent speech in favour of creating a new centre party in British politics.

The Labour right organized itself within the Manifesto Group, formed to defend the Party leadership's right to decide upon the manifesto. It fought, successfully, at the 1980 Party Conference, to reverse the decision taken at the 1979 Conference. Now, both the Party leadership and the Parliamentary Labour Party were to have their control over the manifesto restored. Yet there were reversals for the Labour right in other areas for the 1980 Party Conference also decided to set up an electoral college, bringing together the trade unions, MPs and constituency parties in the election of the Party Leader. The final details of this decision were agreed at Special Labour Party Conference at Wembley in January 1981. Here it was decided to give the trade unions 40 per cent of the vote, the constituency parties 30 per cent and the MPs 30 per cent of the vote in the electoral college.

In October 1980, before the Special Conference occurred, James Callaghan announced his resignation as Labour Leader. He thus forced a leadership contest through the vote of the Labour MPs – the traditional means of selection. Callaghan was replaced by Michael Foot, who defeated Denis Healey in the leadership contest in November 1980 by 139 to 129 votes in the second ballot.

Michael Foot's election indicated that the Party was moving leftwards, since his credentials were very much associated with *Tribune* and other soft left-wing organizations. This was the final straw for the disaffected Labour right. In January 1981, shortly after Foot's election, the Council for Social Democracy was formed at Limehouse, London, by four prominent Labour right-wingers – Roy Jenkins, David Owen, Shirley Williams and Bill Rodgers. This 'Gang of Four' attracted former Labour MPs and activists, such as David Marquand, and separated from the Labour Party an important element who, with the Liberals, appeared by 1982 – or at least before the Falklands War – to present a serious political challenge to both the Conservatives, running low in the polls because of the economic depression, and the Labour Party, also running low in the polls because of their obvious political divisions. Shirley Williams left the NEC of the Labour Party in February 1981 and the Social Democratic Party (SDP) was formed in March 1981. Initially, twelve Labour MPs and nine Labour peers joined the SDP, and eventually a total of twenty-nine Labour MPs joined – all drawn from the eighty-strong right-wing Manifesto Group. This was a serious blow to the Labour right and the Labour Party as a whole. The situation was worsened in September 1982 with the formation of the Liberal–SDP Alliance which, thereafter, posed a serious challenge to the Labour Party.

Those members of the Labour right who did not leave with the Social Democrats organized themselves into the Solidarity group, led by Roy Hattersley, in February 1981 to counter the Labour left. This ensured continuing conflict within the Party and, in April 1981, Tony Benn declared his intention to challenge Denis Healey for the Deputy Leadership of the Party. He failed narrowly, by 50.43 per cent to 49.57 per cent, to win the contest in September 1981 – obtaining the support of the Labour left and a good proportion of the trade-union vote, while Healey won more support among the Parliamentary Labour Party. Had Neil Kinnock, and several other left-wing MPs not abstained it is likely that Healey would have been defeated and the Labour Party might have been even more divided and faced with more defections. Indeed, Giles Radice, a prominent Labour MP of the Labour right, wrote in his diary that 'By beating Benn, however narrowly, Denis Healey saved the Labour Party.'[3] He was probably correct.

According to Healey, his victory was, indeed, the turning point when the Labour right began to reassert itself against the Labour left. In 1980 and 1981, for instance, the left lost seven members on the National Executive Committee of the Labour Party to the right, and right domination has been a feature of the Party ever since. In 1982, as well, Michael Foot was forced into an unsuccessful move to remove the supporters of Militant Tendency.

Indeed, the early 1980s was a period when the Labour Party was faced with a serious level of entryism (joining the Labour Party to subvert its policies and capture influential positions in order to challenge reformism and establish revolutionary socialism) by Militant Tendency, a revolutionary Trotskyist group committed to a vast programme of public ownership whose supporters purchased the weekly newspaper *Militant*. Using constituency Labour parties, the Militant Tendency supporters worked to obtain influence, particularly with the active younger members of the Party.[4] The Labour Party attempted to remove members of Militant Tendency, even though Militant claimed to have no individual members. Foot's campaign failed and, eventually, two Militant supporters – Terry Fields and Dave Nellist – were elected as Labour MPs in the 1983 general election. In addition, Militant supporters won control of the Labour group on Liverpool City Council, led by Derek Hatton. Labour's failure to remove Militant Tendency until the mid-1980s ensured that the majority of the electorate saw Labour as too dangerous a party to return to office.

The political situation swung even further against Labour in 1982 when Margaret Thatcher mounted the Falklands military campaign following the invasion of the Falkland islands by Argentina's armed forces. As the campaign progressed, Labour, despite giving grudging support to the British military campaign, lost ground to the Conservatives. The feeling that Labour lacked a strong sense of patriotic commitment developed further when, at the Labour Party Conference, in October 1982, a substantial majority voted in favour of unilateral disarmament. This reversed the multilateral policy which Gaitskell had won at a Party Conference more than twenty years before.

Associated with one unpopular policy, unilateralism, Labour was also identified with another political liability, the trade unions. Michael Foot attempted to repair the relations with the trade unions which had been strained by the unsuccessful attempt to operate the Social Contract in the mid- and late 1970s. In December 1979, a TUC–Labour Party liaison committee promised to repeal the Conservative employment legislation which was challenging the picketing and strike rights of trade unions. In addition, as already indicated, trade unions were given a 40 per cent vote in the electoral college which selected both the Leader and Deputy Leader of the Labour Party. Perhaps most important of all, a joint TUC and Labour Party document, *Partners in Rebuilding Britain*, agreed that statutory incomes policies would be rejected by a future Labour government in favour of an annual income assessment based upon an agreement between the government, the trade unions and the employers. It is clear that Labour had sought to repair its old links with the trade unions, although one must reflect that trade unions were being weakened by Thatcher's Conservative government and that trade-union membership had declined from more than 12 million in 1979 to about 10.5 million by 1983.[5]

The Labour Party was also still sharply divided on the issue of nationalization. Given the shifting sands of Labour politics one should not expect that there would be consistency of approach. Indeed, there is much evidence that demands for more nationalization from the Labour left would be countered by resistance and occasional victories from the Labour right. There was never a clear majority for a new programme of nationalization and Tony Benn's demand, in May 1980, that public ownership should be extended and that industries privatized by the Conservative government should be renationalized carried limited support and conviction in Party ranks. In 1982, even Michael Foot criticized Benn for advocating the nationalization of the oil industry without compensation. On balance, and excluding Militant Tendency, it seems clear that the majority of the Party was opposed to the idea of further nationalization.

It was, therefore, a divided though more left-wing Labour Party, led by Michael Foot and Denis Healey, closely tied to a diminishing trade-union base, perceived not to be particularly patriotic over the Falklands war, that fought the 1983 general election campaign in June 1983. Its election manifesto *The New Hope for Britain*, drawn up largely by the NEC rather than the Shadow Cabinet, in 1982, still reflected the interests of the declining Labour left. It made sweeping promises to reverse unemployment, which had risen from more than 1 million to more than 3 million during Thatcher's first administration, with an 'emergency programme for action'. It further offered to repeal Conservative trade-union legislation, increase benefits, extend the rights of women and ethnic minorities, to accept unilateral disarmament, and to restore to the public sector, at purchase price, all those industries privatized by the Thatcher government. It also promised to prepare schemes for improving the relations between the trade unions and the Labour Party/government by creating the National Economic Assessment, which would promote planning and industrial democracy.

This policy, formulated by the Labour left, was now put forward by an increasingly right-wing NEC and upon a Shadow Cabinet which had had little chance to discuss it. There were many members of the Labour right who objected to the 1983 manifesto and Geoffrey Bish, the Party's Research Secretary, later reflected that 'The Shadow Cabinet clearly felt that they had been bounced into accepting a document they did not want. They did not like the policies and it showed.'[6] Gerald Kaufmann's comment, already mentioned, that it was 'the longest suicide note in history', was correct for the Labour Party did enormously badly and, with 27.6 per cent of the vote, was a mere 1.6 per cent ahead of the Liberal–SDP Alliance vote. Labour had reached its low point. The switch to the left had not worked. A radical rethink of direction was urgently required.

1983–7: Kinnock, Hattersley and Gradual Reform

Labour's revival was a slow and painstaking process and took several years to move into full gear. It began with a change of leadership, following the resignation of Michael Foot. In October 1983, Neil Kinnock defeated Roy Hattersley, Eric Heffer and Peter Shore in the leadership election; Kinnock won in the third ballot with 71 per cent of the votes to the 19 per cent won by Hattersley. Hattersley eventually became Deputy Leader of the Labour Party and the so-called 'dream ticket', uniting the Labour left and the Labour right was formed. In fact, Kinnock proved rather less left wing than was supposed.

Kinnock had entered Parliament in 1970 and had become a member of the NEC in 1977, where he voted with the Labour left on most issues. However, in 1981 he abstained in the deputy leadership contest, objecting to Benn's candidature. Once elected as Party Leader in 1983, Kinnock began to move the Labour Party to the middle ground in order to recapture the support it had lost in the previous two general elections. Yet moves in that direction were inevitably slow for while his Shadow Cabinet favoured this approach it was the NEC, where the Labour left still held significant influence, that was still shaping Party decisions.

None the less, the creation of a number of joint NEC–Shadow Cabinet policy committees, in 1984, allowed Kinnock to press forward policies in the direction of moderation. The influence of the left was also challenged further when Kinnock moved to change the mandatory re-selection of MPs during the lifetime of each Parliament. The existing system, based upon the constituencies, allowed a small number of activists to challenge, remove and influence the Labour MPs and Kinnock suggested the need to introduce 'One Member One Vote' (OMOV) in place of the block vote influence of trade unions, into the deselection of MPs. The proposal was rejected by about 4 million votes to 3 million at the 1984 Labour Party Conference, but the principle remained part of Kinnock's agenda.

The move towards reform and moderation was set back further in 1984 and 1985 with the protracted miners' strike and the decision of the Conservative government to 'rate cap', by setting limits on the spending of town and city councils. The second of these developments saw Ken Livingstone of the Greater London Council, Ted Knight of Lambeth and David Blunkett of Sheffield City Council jointly defying the government by refusing to set a rate (the tactic of 'non-compliance') in 1985. However, it was Thatcher's attack upon the trade unions, particularly on the National Union of Mineworkers (NUM) and coal miners, that caused the biggest problem.

The 1984/5 national coal strike began on 9 March 1984 at the pits in Scotland and Yorkshire, where the National Coal Board (NCB) had decided to cut coal output and employment in the mines. However, the NUM decided that there was to be no national ballot. The NUM also sent flying pickets from Yorkshire to Scotland, Nottingham and Kent to persuade working miners to join the dispute, despite the High Court injunction forbidding such action.[7] This led to mass picketing and violence, notably at Ollerton in Nottinghamshire, where a Yorkshire miner was crushed to death in the demonstrations outside the pit, and later at the Orgreave coke plant. There were many twists and turns throughout the dispute. On 14 March 1984 the High Court gave the NCB an injunction against the flying pickets, though the NCB chose not to use it. The government also maintained a police presence to stop the movement of flying pickets.

As the strike ground on, the court action began to take effect. The South Wales Mineworkers were fined £50,000 for contempt over picketing and when this was not paid the sequestrators seized their funds of £707,000. The NUM was also fined £200,000 on 10 October for breaking an order declaring the strike to be unofficial, and when it also failed to pay its assets were seized.

There was much violence and many incidents of high emotion during the strike, one of the most famous being the dropping of a cement block from a motorway bridge on to a taxi taking a miner to work in South Wales, killing the driver and leading to two strikers each being sent to gaol for 20 years. Eventually, the strike came to an end, in a ragged fashion, and without any settlement, when a special delegate meeting of the mineworkers decided to return to work without agreement on 3 March 1985.

The violence associated with that 1984/5 miners' strike was used to discredit the Labour Party by Thatcher's Conservative government. Also, despite the mixed feelings of some trade unionists, Arthur Scargill, the President of the NUM, drew immense personal support at the 1984 TUC Conference. Kinnock was, therefore, faced with a mixture of reaction and radicalism which threatened to blow off course his attempt to give the Labour Party an image of moderation.

To deal with these challenges, Kinnock attempted to distance himself, and the Labour Party, from the conflict. He criticized the embarrassing tactics of Arthur Scargill in not calling for a national strike ballot before calling strike action. In June 1984 he further criticized the violence of both the police and the pickets and in October 1984 attacked the confrontational tactics of the NUM. This was despite the fact that Scargill received a standing ovation when he spoke to the Labour Party Conference of October 1985, which produced the tellingly hostile photograph of Kinnock looking over the shoulder of Scargill as he was making his speech. In January 1985, Kinnock criticized Arthur Scargill for acting like a First World War general in relation to the troops, in a clear reference to the comment that the situation was one of 'heroes led by donkeys'. In March 1985, Kinnock further refused to commit any future Labour government to giving amnesty to any miner convicted of serious crime, a commitment requested by the NUM. The final throw of the dice was Kinnock's attack upon Scargill's conduct of the strike made at the Labour Party Conference in October 1985.

Both the non-compliance protest and the miners' strike eventually disintegrated. But they left the Labour Party identified with the extreme Labour left, something which Kinnock had tried to avoid with his criticism of Scargill's tactics. Kinnock clearly wished to distance himself from the type of trade union and industrial action which had brought Labour into political disfavour in the 'winter of discontent' of 1979 and which had undermined Labour's fortunes in the early 1980s. The miners' strike had not provided him with much of an opportunity for this but his attempt to remove the Militant Tendency faction proved a more effective means of creating the image of Labour as a party of political moderation.

At the 1985 Labour Party Conference, Kinnock was extremely critical of Derek Hatton, leader of the Militant Tendency faction that ran Liverpool City Council. He was particularly appalled at the action of the Militant Tendency leaders in Liverpool in issuing redundancy notices to all its city council in order to place pressure on the Thatcher government to remove its capping of council expenditure. This had annoyed the trade unions and at the Conference Kinnock stated that

> I'll tell you what happens with impossible promises. You start with far-fetched revolutions. You are then pickled into a rigid dogma, a code, and you go through the years sticking to that, outdated, misplaced, irrelevant to the real needs, and you end in the grotesque chaos of a Labour council hiring taxis to scuttle round a city handing out redundancy notices to its own workers. [Applause] . . . You can't play politics with people's jobs . . . [Applause and some boos].[8]

One front bench Labour MP was heard to say that 'with one speech he [Kinnock] lanced the boil'.[9]

Indeed, the National Executive Committee began an investigation into the Liverpool Labour Party which, in March 1986, was surcharged by the High Court, along with Lambeth Council, for not setting a council rate on time as directed by the Thatcher government. The National Executive Committee of the Labour Party later, at the 1986 Labour Party Conference, recommended that the Liverpool District Party be expelled.

By his actions, Kinnock was beginning to unite the Labour right with the soft left of the Party, represented by David Blunkett, Michael Meacher and the Tribune Group within the NEC. He also alienated and isolated the hard left, the Trotskyists, the Campaign for Labour Party Democracy and related bodies. Yet to present Labour as a party of moderation also required changes in its policy commitments – particularly on the three major policy areas of nationalization, industrial relations and unilateral nuclear disarmament.

Kinnock began to move the Party away from its commitment to nationalization in 1985, when he declared that the renationalization of industries privatized by the Conservative government would not be a priority for a future Labour government. The Deputy Leader, Roy Hattersley, re-emphasized this point when his proposals for a variety of forms of social ownership, rather than nationalization, were accepted at the Party Conference in 1985. The unifying symbol of Labour's socialism of 1918, challenged in the 1950s by Gaitskell was now, once again, being challenged, for pragmatic reasons, by Kinnock and Hattersley. Yet Kinnock, in order to keep the soft left on board with his political agenda, accepted that there would be a compromise arrangement whereby British Gas and British Telecom, both recently privatized organizations, would be returned to public control with compensation.

Kinnock also wanted Labour to be further distanced from the industrial action which had blighted its fortunes in 1979. He wished to retain much of the new framework of the Conservative government's industrial legislation but eventually compromised upon repealing the existing framework while insisting that ballots would be held on strikes and that trade-union executives would have to have their position constantly reaffirmed.[10]

On the issue of unilateralism, however, Kinnock faced his sternest opposition. The issue had almost become the mark of being a socialist and the policy had been restated at the 1984 Party Conference. By 1986, Kinnock was receiving evidence that unilateralism was a vote loser. Unable to influence the Party on this issue, by December 1986 Kinnock was suggesting that a non-nuclear policy would be a step to developing NATO's strategy and would release savings for social spending.[11] There was little evidence that this cut any ice with the British public.

The first four years of Kinnock's leadership were thus eventful ones in which he tried to allay the fears of the British public that the Labour

Party was irresponsible and too politically extreme. This strategy had been particularly focused against industrial action and Militant Tendency. Nevertheless, the Party remained committed to unilateral disarmament, still seen as a rather extreme policy, and reiterated its belief in a non-nuclear defence policy at the 1985 Labour Party Conference. It also voted for the removal of United States nuclear bases from Britain at the 1986 Labour Party Conference. Even further, in March 1987 Kinnock also committed a future Labour government to the instant withdrawal of the Polaris nuclear submarines from patrol.

Given these policies it was inevitable that the Labour Party would be subject to press criticism. Indeed, the press began a campaign against Labour which exposed to ridicule all its policies, including those connected with gay and Green (environmental) issues, during the Greenwich parliamentary by-election of March 1987 when a hard-left candidate was defeated by a SDP candidate. Labour's popularity declined and the campaign culminated in a leaked letter from Patricia Hewitt, Kinnock's press secretary, who wrote that 'It's obvious from our polling, as well as from the doorstep that . . . the 'loony' Labour left is taking its toll; the gays and lesbian issue is costing us dear amongst the pensioners, the fear of extremism and higher tax/rates is particularly prominent in the GLC area. . . .'[12] The omens were not good for the forthcoming general election.

As Labour geared up to the 1987 general election it began to focus upon the need to reverse the tax cuts of the Conservatives, which favoured the better-off sections of society, and to stimulate investment through a British Investment Bank in its policy document *New Industrial Strength for Britain* (1987). Then in the June 1987 general election Labour conducted a most impressive political campaign with its manifesto *Britain Will Win*. Yet Labour was, once again, defeated although there was some recovery from the debacle of the 1983 general election. It was particularly successful in both Scotland and the north of England but still only won 30.8 per cent of the vote and 229 seats.

Labour's campaign appears to have been derailed by two issues: those of defence and taxation. On defence, Labour was misrepresented as being committed to pacifism, with one advert depicting 'Labour's policy on arms' as being a soldier with his hands in the air. On taxation, the Conservative treasury ministers costed Labour's election pledges at £35 billion and thus responsible for crippling levels of taxation if implemented.

KINNOCK AND THE SPEEDING UP OF REFORM 1987–92

In many respects Labour's election defeat speeded up the process of reform which ended in the politics of New Labour and 'Blairism', even if Kinnock and Hattersley never contemplated going as far as Blair later did in totally redefining the socialism of the Labour Party and rejecting the role of the state in maintaining full employment. Nevertheless, Neil Kinnock began a course of action between 1987 and 1992 which was designed to remove the image of Labour both as an extremist and divided party.[13] The starting point, in many respects, was the Labour Party Conference of September 1987, which overwhelmingly endorsed Neil Kinnock's decision to review the entire range of Labour's policies. The inevitable meaning of this was that more moderate political policies would emerge. Indeed, the Policy Review was designed to create 'a more moderate social democratic party – accepting the role of the market, dropping the commitment to unilateralism and opening the door for constitutional reform'.[14]

Between 1988 and 1991, four Policy Review reports were published. The first, *Social Justice and Economic Efficiency* was a vague statement of aims and carried little impact. The second, *Meet the Challenge and Make the Change* was submitted to, and accepted by, the 1989 Labour Party Conference. The third, *Looking to the Future* suggested a rightward move as did the fourth, *Opportunity Britain*, which was presented to the 1991 Labour Party Conference. These four reports formed the basis for the Labour Party's 1992 manifesto *It's Time to Get Britain Working Again*.

These reports. collectively, abandoned many of Labour's established shibboleths. Labour's commitment to public ownership was played down, particularly in *Meet the Challenge, Make the Change*, where it was suggested that private industry would have an important part to play in Britain's future society. Labour's commitment to intervene in the workings of the City of London, put forward by Bryan Gould who convened the economic group of the Policy Review, was also watered down when he was replaced as industry spokesman by Gordon Brown. There was going to be no future commitment by Labour to further nationalization, although there remained the problem of the privatization measures which the Thatcher and Major governments had introduced. *Looking to the Future* (page 17) did suggest that Labour would take back ownership of the water companies but even this was reduced to the issue of control by the time of the 1992 manifesto.

In effect, by 1992 Labour had abandoned the idea of state interventionism, and public ownership, and had also abandoned the idea of pumping money into and out of the economy in the classic Keynesian desire to respond to economic slumps and booms. It had linked itself to the need for a fixed and high exchange rate, with all the deflationary pressures and consequences that had resulted in the Thatcher era, as a means of regulating the economy. Thus Labour's commitment to full employment was ended. Its commitment to social welfare provision was, therefore, also played down. The general election of 1987, and additional research at that time, suggested that the British public were not prepared to accept high taxation. Consequently, Labour's attempt to influence the supply of goods and services would have to be abandoned if it was to win wide political support. The Labour Party accepted this situation, which effectively meant that it made limited commitment to increasing family allowances and pensions at the 1992 general election. Public expenditure was to be stringently controlled, as John Smith, Labour's Shadow Chancellor, stated 'we can't spend what we haven't earned. We intend to earn it before we can spend it. That will be the guiding light of the next Labour government's economic policy.'[15] Even the minimalist social-security welfare state that Britain had adopted was going to be restrained.

The Policy Review also tackled the thorny issues of trade unions and defence. On trade unionism, Labour had already indicated that some, perhaps much, of the Thatcher legislation would be retained and Tony Blair, who took over from Michael Meacher as front-bench spokesman on Employment and convenor of the industrial relations Policy Review in October 1989, ensured that much of the Thatcher legislation, including the banning of the closed shop system (whereby only trade-union members would be employed), would be retained while allowing picketing and secondary picketing under specific legally defined circumstances. The 1992 Labour manifesto thus stated that 'there will be no return to the trade-union legislation of the 1970s. . . . There will be no mass or flying pickets.'[16]

On defence, Kinnock ensured that the Policy Review Group was dominated by anti-unilateralists and its report was compiled by Gerald Kaufmann, the Shadow Foreign Secretary. This report suggested that Labour should drop its unilateral stance and Kinnock endorsed it, indicating that he would resign if the new line was not supported at Party Conference. Obviously, the Labour Party Conference of 1990 endorsed his position, stressing that Britain would reduce her nuclear capacity through multilateral agreements. The 1992 manifesto confirmed this

Kinnock also managed to get the principle of 'one member, one vote' (OMOV) accepted. The NEC of the Labour Party suggested that the principle be used in the voting in the leadership and deputy leadership contests in 1988 and recommended the principle in its own elections from 1989 for its own constituency sections. What is clear is that Kinnock was able to push forward with his reforms to such an extent that the Labour left became marginalized. Indeed, with the changes came an increasingly right-wing dominated NEC which now supported Kinnock, in a way in which its left-wing influence, had not allowed it to operate between the late 1970s and the mid-1980s. The NEC of the Labour Party was now operating, once again, in line with the Party leadership and the Parliamentary Labour Party. Unified on organization, and unified on a more moderate policy, Labour now had some prospect of political success.

There were growing signs that the strategy of moderation was working. Labour continued to do well in the municipal elections and, in May 1989, Labour won forty-five seats in the elections for the European Parliament, in contrast to the thirty-one seats won by the Conservatives. This was Thatcher's first major political reversal at the national level and all the more surprising since Labour was still committed to its 1983 pledge to withdraw from the EEC. This was also at a time when Kinnock welcomed the EEC's commitment to a social charter, of rights for workers, which had just been drafted by the French socialist Jacques Delors.

Nevertheless, Labour still lagged in the polls and, in September 1991, on the eve of the Labour Party Conference, there was much press rumour that Kinnock was under pressure to resign in order to improve Labour's electoral prospects. Kinnock denied that there were such pressures and prepared the way for the general election of 1992.

Since Labour had improved its position in the 1987 general election there was great optimism that it would end its political wilderness years at the 1992 general election, in spite of opinion polls flagging as the election day approached. In March/April 1992 it issued its general election manifesto, *It's Time to Get Britain Working Again*, which promised an extra £1,000 million for the National Health Service, £600 million for education, increases in retirement pensions and child benefits, a minimum wage of £3.40 an hour, a 50 per cent higher rate of income tax, the abolition of the National Insurance ceiling, which would have greatly increased the National Insurance contributions of high earners, and the replacement of the House of Lords with an elected second chamber.

Unfortunately for Labour, of course, it became embroiled in a debate about the costing of its reforms and the suggestion that its taxes, which were to rise from 40 per cent to 50 per cent for the higher tax payers, would be insufficient to pay for its reforms. Indeed, Labour's specific proposals and tax policies were attacked by the Conservative Party and the media to frighten potential Labour voters, with talk of Labour's 'tax bombshell'.

Nevertheless, the Labour Party was clearly in high spirits for the 1992 general election. It had effectively removed its unpopular policies of nationalization and unilateral disarmament. The Liberal–SDP Alliance of 1987 had been engulfed by a rampant Green Party, which pushed it down to fourth in the opinion polls on the eve of the election. The political time looked ripe for Labour's political revival. Yet the Party lost. It has been suggested that this defeat had little to do with Labour's Policy Review, for most electors recognized that 'Labour was now more moderate'.[18] It has also been suggested that Kinnock's leadership was the reason for the defeat. According to one report 'Mr Major did not win the election. Mr Kinnock lost it.'[19] Another said 'Voters just did not believe Mr Kinnock was fit to run Britain',[20] while yet another argued that the task of winning the election was just 'too much for a man who had to spend time inventing a new identity for himself'.[21] None the less, recent research indicates that there is little evidence to maintain that the quality, or perceived quality, of leadership has much to do with electoral success for while the Labour leadership can make some minor impact upon elections its influence is seldom decisive.[22]

It is not easy to establish precisely why Labour lost. Perhaps it was partly to do with a diminished trade-union and traditional working-class base for Labour, some minor uncertainty about Kinnock's leadership or some concern about the extent to which Labour had become more moderate. Yet there were, possibly, other factors. Generally, the newspapers campaigned against Labour and exposed its shortcomings and mistakes. In particular, they made great play of the problems with the Labour Party's Shadow Budget, as already indicated, and campaigns such as the 'War of Jennifer's Ear' and the over-confident, and highly triumphalist, rally that was held at Sheffield Arena.

The 'War of Jennifer's Ear' had begun on 24 March 1992, when a Labour Party television election broadcast focused upon two girls with ear problems one of whom had an immediate operation through private medicine and the other, Jennifer Bennett, whose operation was delayed because she was an NHS patient. There then followed a massive Tory campaign which suggested that Labour had been responsible for a Goebbels-like 'Big Lie' and a debate when Jennifer's consultant suggested that her delay was due to medical rather than resource deficiencies. This was denied by Jennifer's father who indicated that the consultant had told him that the delay was due to limited resources.[23] The affair undoubtedly distracted the electorate from the real issues being fought.

Equally off-putting may have been the self-confidence that Labour exuded in the run-up to the general election. On 1 April 1992 the Labour Party held its 'glitzy rally' at Sheffield Arena, which conveyed the impression of a Party on the eve of victory.[24] Widely covered by the press, there seems to have been a negative reaction to it from among the electorate.

Yet media events, such as Jennifer's Ear and the Sheffield Arena rally, were topped by the *Sun*'s open advice, on 9 April, for the electors to vote for the Conservatives asking, 'in the event of a Labour victory will the last person to leave the UK please switch off the light'. Rupert Murdoch, owner of the paper most widely read by the working class, had declared strongly against Labour and certainly did influence the undecided voters. Indeed, the *Sun* claimed, on 10 April 1992, that it was 'the *Sun* wot won it'. It is uncertain if this was the case but what is clear is that the Labour Party lost again, winning only 271 seats.

1992–4: JOHN SMITH AND THE CHANGING IMAGE OF LABOUR

In the immediate wake of defeat both Neil Kinnock and Roy Hattersley signalled their intention to resign. John Smith was elected as Labour Leader in July 1992, overwhelmingly defeating Bryan Gould by 91 per cent to 9 per cent in the leadership contest. Margaret Beckett was elected Deputy Leader with 57 per cent of the vote against the 28 per cent of John Prescott and the 14.5 per cent of Bryan Gould.

Smith was fifty-four years of age at the time of his election and had been a Labour MP since 1970, first of all for Lanarkshire North and then for Monklands East. He had been a Minister of State in the 1970s, eventually becoming Secretary of State for Trade in 1978. A sharp and shrewd economist he had been Shadow Chancellor of the Exchequer during the 1992 general election, being largely responsible for the much vilified Shadow Budget, which had spelled out how Labour would raise the money for its electoral promises. As Leader of the Labour Party he adopted a conciliatory tone in order to keep all sides of the Party in tolerable unison and promised to reform the relationship between the Party and the trade unions by abolishing the union block vote at Party Conferences. Indeed, in September 1992 the Labour Party Conference did reduce the strength of trade-union delegates' votes from 90 per cent to 70 per cent, but retained union participation in leadership elections and the selection of candidates.

This attempt to weaken the trade-union stranglehold on the Party went further in February 1993 when Smith proposed to reduce the unions' share of the vote in leadership elections, which had been 40 per cent, and the selection of candidates at constituency level. The following September, the Party Conference agreed to the introduction of 'one member one vote' (OMOV), by which the trade-union and constituency party sections of the electoral college were forced to ballot members individually for the Party Leader and the Deputy Leader elections and to allocate the votes proportionally. The trade unions, MPs and the constituencies were also given one-third each of the vote in the electoral college. The electorate for the Labour leadership contests now numbered millions, not a few hundred or thousand activists in smoke-filled committee rooms.

The selection of Labour's candidates for Parliament proved more troublesome. There was strong support for the OMOV principle but the trade unions and the constituency parties wished to retain their control over selection. John Prescott came up with a compromise arrangement, the 'levy-plus' scheme whereby political levy payers could participate in selections if they joined the Party at a discounted rate. The proposal was approved by the NEC in July 1993 but fought out during the summer months between the 'modernizers' in the Party and the trade unions, who suspected that the Labour Party would break its trade-union link once a Labour government was able to obtain state funding for political parties. In the end, and only after a dramatic speech by Prescott, the 1993 Labour Party Conference agreed to the proposal by 47.5 per cent to 44.4 per cent. There was now, theoretically, more power for the individual party member and less for the institutional power of trade unions.

Yet almost before Smith had begun his reforms he was gone. He died suddenly in May 1994, of a heart attack, and it appeared that Labour would now be set back in its reforming agenda. However, in July 1994, Tony Blair was elected Leader of the Labour Party with John Prescott elected as his Deputy. Within months, rather than years, Labour was moving more rapidly to ditching the old Labour shibboleths, most obviously nationalization, for good, and moving towards what has become known as New Labour, or the politics of the Third Way.

CONCLUSION

The Labour Party was out of office between 1979 and 1994, and had to wait another three years before it won a general election. At first it had sought to win back its traditional working-class support through a reliance upon its old trade-union connections, a commitment to further nationalization and unilateral disarmament. After 1983, when the Labour Party received its biggest drubbing in a parliamentary election since 1931, it became clear that Labour's leaders – Neil Kinnock, John Smith and, temporarily in 1994, Margaret Beckett – would move Labour away from the policies of the left. What Kinnock did was weaken trade-union power within the Labour Party, reject the policy of unilateral disarmament and abandon nationalization as the linchpins of a future Labour Party. Recognizing that the traditional industrial base of the Labour Party was declining rapidly, Kinnock, by 1987, had set Labour on the course to becoming a social democratic party, not that much different from the one that was formed by Labour's dissident right-wing MPs in 1981. By 1994, Labour seemed to be nearer to the point of forming a government than it had been since 1979, and to have recovered most of the political ground it had lost in the 1983 general election. With the election of Blair it is clear that Labour had a Leader who might win the next general election. Teresa Gorman, the Conservative MP, recognized and feared this in June 1994, before the election, hoping that Prescott would win. Indeed, she proved correct for she saw in Blair a Labour Leader, not of the traditional mould, who was determined to win a broader range of support for Labour.[25]

CHAPTER EIGHT

New Labour and Labour in Government, 1994–2000

Tony Blair, perhaps more than any other Labour Leader, has been the modernizer who has not had to look to the past. Most other Labour Leaders – MacDonald, Attlee, Gaitskell, Wilson, Callaghan, Foot, Kinnock, and even Smith – have had to assimilate the past culture of Labour, steeped in the trade-union traditions and collectivism of the past. Blair, following through the ideas of his mentor Neil Kinnock, was determined not to be constricted by the Old Labour culture. He felt that change was now more necessary than ever since the traditional mass industrial techniques had given way to a lighter more service-oriented type of industry. The traditional working-class workforce had changed enormously and declined. Blair accepted that the Conservative Party had been successful since it was seen as the party that opposed state control and that Labour was seen as the party linked with trade unionism, the state, ethnic minorities and social security claimants. Such perceptions, whether real or exaggerated, had to be changed. The 'New Labour' Party Blair was to lead needed to cultivate the moderate image which Kinnock had been pressing for in the 1980s and in the early 1990s.[1] It needed to accept some of the changes that the Conservatives had introduced and to convince voters that it would not raise taxes, favour the trade unions, overspend and build up debts. In other words, it had to remove the demons of 'Old Labour'.

CLAUSE FOUR AND THE EVOLUTION OF 'NEW LABOUR'

The symbol of this change from 'Old Labour' to 'New Labour' was the removal of the traditional Clause Four of the Labour Party Constitution, which committed Labour to the common ownership of the means of production. Giles Radice and Steve Pollard, two modernizers, suggested that such an action was essential for Labour's political future.[2] A year later Blair announced his intention to reject the old Clause Four at the 1994 Labour Party Conference, and praised the successes of capitalism. Soon afterwards, he presented his alternative Clause Four, which, after amendments, was accepted by the National Executive Committee of the Labour Party. It committed Labour 'to work for a dynamic economy, serving the public interest, in which the enterprise of the market and the rigour of competition are joined with the forces of partnership and cooperation . . . with a thriving sector and high quality public services . . . '. In addition, there were vague references to a just society, security against fear, equality of opportunity and other related issues. This new Clause Four was to replace the existing one which had been the basis of Labour's commitment to social justice, equality and full employment. Effectively, the idea of redistribution of wealth and income within British society was being rejected. The race was now on to get this accepted by the Party as a whole.

At first it appeared that constituencies and trade unions would be against the change and so, at the end of 1994, Blair held an intensive round of meetings where he personally appealed to 30,000 Party members to support his new Clause Four. There was stern trade-union opposition to the new version, particularly from the Transport and General Workers' Union, but, with more than two-thirds of the constituency Labour parties deciding to ballot their members, it was clear that about 85 per cent of their members would support Blair's new Clause Four.

At a special conference of the Labour Party held on 29 April 1995, which was seen by the press as a test of Blair's ability to deal effectively with the trade unions, he won support for his new Clause Four by just under two-thirds of the vote. This revealed that 54.6 per cent of the 70 per cent union vote and about 90 per cent of the 30 per cent constituency vote had supported Blair.[3] Effectively, Blair had won support for his reforming leadership of the Labour Party, and the press and media recognized that this had been his personal triumph. He had tackled and tamed trade-union opposition, buoyed up by the recognition that he and the Labour Party would not be taken seriously by the public if the proposal had been defeated. In the end, the majority of trade unions and constituency parties dared not vote against Blair if they wished the Party to have a significant political future. Their comfort was that Blair and the Labour Party made concessions in other directions to offset their doubts, most notably in moving the Labour Party Conference of October

1996 to vote in favour of the European Social Charter by 1 January 1998 (following through on Kinnock's support for it in 1989), advocating the introduction of the minimum wage, and agreeing to end the internal competitive market in the National Health Service, which had been introduced by Thatcher and Major.

'New Labour' has now rejected the old Keynesian social democracy of the 'Old', which had suggested that the state could intervene to promote growth and thus ensure economic growth and employment. Instead, it was now committed to the pursuit of low inflation, through the increased powers of the Bank of England and prepared to use interest rates in the same fashion as the Thatcher and Major governments had done.[4] This meant that increased tax rates were ruled out and that Labour's past commitment to redistributing income and wealth was at an end.

These views were confirmed in a book written by Peter Mandelson and Roger Liddle entitled *The Blair Revolution: Can New Labour Deliver*, written in 1996. It suggested that Labour was standing on the brink of power and outlined the type of society that New Labour wished to create. Mandelson had been long involved in the development of the New Labour strategy. He became MP for Hartlepool in 1992 and was, previously, Party Director of the Campaigns and Communications, between 1985 and 1990 while Neil Kinnock was Labour's Leader. He had previously been a television producer between 1982 and 1985. Mandelson was steeped in the arts of the media and public relations. So was Roger Liddle, who was the managing director of PRIMA Europe, a body of public policy consultants. He had previously been an adviser in the Callaghan government, and had left Labour to join the SDP before returning to the Labour Party, becoming one of Tony Blair's policy advisers. These were two of the so-called 'spin doctors' (media manipulators) of 'New Labour'.

Their lengthy and detailed book covered every aspect of New Labour's policy in building up a new society in Britain by 2005. It suggested that

> New Labour has set itself a bold task: to modernise Britain socially, economically and politically. In doing so it aims to build on Britain's strengths. Its mission is to create not to destroy. Its strategy is to move forward from where Margaret Thatcher left off, rather than to dismantle every single thing she did.[5]

It then suggested that New Labour's approach was based upon five insights: the need for people to feel secure; investment, partnership and top quality education for all; the recognition of the potential of government; and 'One Nation socialism' going beyond the battles of the past between private and public interests; and, further, the need to unite public and private activities in the ideal of social cooperation.[6] Put more explicitly:

> New Labour believes that it is possible to combine a free-market economy with social justice; liberty of the individual with wider opportunities for all; One Nation security with efficiency and competitiveness; rights with responsibilities, personal self-fulfilment with strengthening the family; effective government and decisive political leadership with a new constitutional settlement and a new relationship of trust between politicians and the people; a love of Britain with a recognition that Britain's future has to lie in Europe.[7]

This is as clear a statement of 'New Labour' as is possible in a mere seventy or so words.

The commitment to partnership between public and private sectors, the 'Third Way', has been the fundamental characteristic of New Labour's general strategy. Despite repeated indications of this in policy, and Blair's willingness to cut across the political barriers for advice and help, it would appear that this was not immediately evident. To the media and the public, Blair was more the man who had stood up to the unions and abandoned nationalization. The more subtle point is his policies; most obviously, the rejection of Keynesian economics, large-scale government intervention and the maintenance of full employment, were not immediately detected. Instead, Blair's personality, charm and communication skills quickly endeared him to the British electorate.

THE GENERAL ELECTION OF 1997

With Blair running high in the opinion polls it is hardly surprising that John Major delayed the 1997 general election to the last possible date. On 1 May 1997 Tony Blair headed a Labour Party to a sweeping victory. With 44.4 per cent of the vote Labour won 419 seats to the Conservatives' 165 (336 in 1992), winning an overall majority of 179 seats. Labour's proportion of the vote was up by 10.8 per cent on 1992. Also, most remarkably, the 122 women MPs in Parliament, more than doubled the number achieved in 1992. With this victory, and these changes, Blair had successfully presented the modernization of the Labour Party as the precursor of the modernization of Britain: 'New Labour, New Britain'.

The 1997 general election returned the Labour Party to office after eighteen years of opposition. The shift of support from the Conservatives to the Labour Party was the biggest this century, in what has been referred to as a landslide victory. But why had this occurred? Was it achieved as a result of Conservative failings, Labour's transformation, or a combination of both factors?

Certainly, the Conservative Party lost 11 per cent of the vote, falling from 42 per cent to 31 per cent, its lowest proportion of the vote since 1832. This was probably a result of its declining influence in the local elections, a product of being in office so long, but also partly the result of the internal wrangling within the party between the pro-Europeans and the Euro-sceptics. This last issue had led John Major to resign as party leader on 22 June 1995, though not as Prime Minister, to force a contest between himself and the Euro-sceptic John Redwood, who resigned from the Cabinet. Subsequently, on 4 July, Major won the contest by 218 votes to 89, with 22 votes not being recorded. Thus the Conservative Party was clearly divided. 'Sleaze' was probably the final straw.

During John Major's last administration, between 1992 and 1997, a number of ministers had been forced to resign because of sexual or financial misconduct. In particular, there were allegations that Conservative MPs were willing to accept money for asking parliamentary questions and this led Major to establish a Committee on Standards in Public Life, chaired by Lord Nolan, a judge. Similar concern over ministers and arms sales to Iraq led to the creation of an inquiry under Lord Justice Scott. By the time of the 1997 general election, the public were already well aware of the sleaze issue which seemed to be engulfing the Conservative government. The most embarrassing situation for them was the publicity given to the accusations against Neil Hamilton throughout the general election campaign.

Neil Hamilton, the former Conservative Minister of Trade, was accused of going beyond legitimate consultancy for the lobbying company Ian Greer Associates, by accepting cash for asking parliamentary questions on behalf of the owner of Harrods, Mohammed Al Fayed. Hamilton began libel proceedings against the *Guardian* for the accusations it had made throughout 1996. At the last moment he withdrew his action. The *Guardian* continued to accuse him, and some other Conservative MPs, of corrupt activities, and Hamilton's position was weakened further when one of his co-accused, Tim Smith, MP for Beaconsfield, resigned as parliamentary candidate after admitting receiving cash from Al Fayed for asking parliamentary questions.[8] The issue came to haunt both the Conservative Party and Hamilton when Martin Bell, the BBC war correspondent, campaigned against Hamilton in his Tatton seat, the fourth safest Conservative seat in the country, and won as an independent candidate.

Events had certainly conspired against the Conservatives at a time when 'New Labour' seemed fresh and innovative, with a popular leader. In the three years up to the election, as indicated, Labour was reducing its commitments to the trade unions and to public ownership and widening its appeal to the middle-class voters. In addition, in order not to be faced with a repeat of the financial fiasco of 1992, when the Shadow Budget discussion had been partly Labour's undoing, Gordon Brown, Labour's Shadow Chancellor of the Exchequer, made a speech in January 1996 promising not to increase the basic rate of income tax, nor increase the higher rate of tax, and not to increase VAT on goods. He further declared Labour's intention to continue with the existing spending plans of the Conservative government for two years and that Labour's extra spending commitments would be paid for out of a 'windfall tax' imposed, as a one-off, upon the privatized industries which had been making massive profits and paying their directors substantial increases, much to the annoyance of the British public. Peter Mandelson stated that Labour could nail 'Tory lies about us on tax and spending'.[9] This speech certainly helped Labour win the general election.

Yet there were also other factors at play. Rupert Murdoch, the owner of the *Sun, The Times, Sunday Times* and the *News of the World* newspapers, threw his weight behind the Labour Party which was reflected in the fact that the *Sun* and the *News of the World* supported the Labour Party. Only the *Sunday Times* was positively a Conservative paper. This certainly reversed the position of the 1992 general election when the Murdoch papers were vehemently opposed to Labour.

Blair was particularly concerned about the Party image and its presentation to the media, to such an extent that Labour rented two floors of Millbank Tower, in Westminster, where Peter Mandelson and about eighty staff operated to present the Labour message more effectively. Eventually, 250 staff were organized into twelve task forces, specializing on particular issues, to respond to and rebut charges made by the Conservative Party. The 'political smart arses' at Millbank, as John Prescott referred to them, ensured that there were few political gaffes.

Labour's campaign went well and their manifesto, *New Labour: Because Britain Deserves Better*, issued on 3 April 1997, proved attractive by offering a ten-point personal contract with the British people, the central aim of which was to improve education. It emerged from the *New Labour: New Life for Britain* document, issued in 1996, which had promised to cut school class sizes for young children; to halve the times between the arrest and punishment of young criminals; to cut the National Health Service waiting lists; to get 250,000 young unemployed back to work; and to set tough rules for future government spending and borrowing.

There were some problems, most obviously the Conservative suggestion that Labour's spending plans would cost £1,500 million more than the available revenue. However, Labour responded to this perceived 'funding gap' by indicating that it would also privatize in order to raise the necessary money.

In the end, Labour's campaign appealed to the upper working-class and middle-class voters throughout the south-east of England, as well as to its traditional support. The failures of the Conservatives and the policies of the Labour Party were enough to win Labour its landslide victory.[10]

1997–2000: THE EARLY YEARS OF BLAIR'S LABOUR GOVERNMENT

Once in office, Blair moved quickly to establish his New Labour credentials. In June 1997 he signed the European Social Charter on Workers' Rights. From the start, he also decided to strengthen the centre of government. Peter Mandelson was appointed Minister without Portfolio inside the Cabinet Office to coordinate the work of government departments, and a strategy committee of the Cabinet was set up under Blair's own chairmanship. The Labour government also introduced a new ministerial code requiring that all media contacts and policy initiatives by ministers should be cleared in advance by Downing Street.

In order to strengthen control further, Blair pressed the Labour Party Conference of 1997 to adopt *Partnership into Power*, a document which set out a radical programme to reform the Party's decision-making processes. By this, the Party Conference lost its control over Party policy to a 175-strong National Party Forum which would discuss policies, in a two-year rolling cycle, and the National Executive Committee (NEC) of the Party was altered. The women's section of the NEC was to be abolished and trade-union representatives reduced from seventeen to twelve, although six were to be women. Three places were to be reserved for members of the Labour government (or Party) and appointed by Tony Blair (Party Leader/Prime Minister) and one for the leader of the Labour Group in the European Parliament. Six were to be set aside for representatives elected by postal ballot of all members. These changes weakened the Labour Party Conference, reduced the power of the trade unions, and strengthened the hand of Tony Blair, as Labour Leader.

Riding upon huge popular support, Blair responded by beginning a variety of initiatives, in a veritable rush of activity. In addition to signing the European Social Charter, Blair offered Sinn Fein a meeting with officials on the Northern Ireland peace process without the precondition of a renewed ceasefire, and in the Queen's Speech to Parliament, the new government set out the commitments to a minimum wage and to constitutional reform. Gordon Brown, the new Chancellor of the Exchequer, also announced that the Bank of England, rather than the government, would take responsibility for setting interest rates through a new monetary policy committee. In June 1997, task forces were established on NHS efficiency and youth justice.

The 'New Labour' approach to the economy was also quickly evident in Gordon Brown's first Budget, in July 1997, with cuts in corporation tax, on businesses, the reduction of VAT on fuel to 5 per cent, cuts in mortgage tax relief and a £5,200 million windfall tax on privatized utilities in order to finance the Welfare to Work programme and to reduce youth and long-term unemployment by 250,000. The 'New Labour' emphasis upon health and education was reflected in a commitment to further spending of £3,500 million. Shortly afterwards, however, it was announced that student grants would be replaced by student loans, as suggested in the (Ron) Dearing Report, the ideas being that money would flow into higher education. The overall New Labour formula was to be increased public spending without increased taxation: the best of both worlds.

New Labour, in applying its new philosophy, has focused five main areas. Firstly, it has sought to communicate with the public and to present a better image of Labour policies than has previously occurred. It has also emphasized that there will be a greater openness in government.

Clement Attlee, Labour's Prime Minister 1945–51, seen here in the late 1930s or early 1940s.

Sir Stafford Cripps, late 1930s.

Herbert Morrison and Aneurin Bevan in unusually good humour at the Labour Party conference at Norwich, 1937.

Left to right: George Brown (Deputy Leader of the Labour Party), Len Williams (General Secretary), Hugh Gaitskell (Leader) and Harold Wilson, walking through Brighton during the Labour Party Conference, on 29 September 1962, at a time when the Party was taking a neutral stand on Britain's possible entry to the European Common Market.

Harold Wilson on a train to his Huyton constituency in a typical pipe-smoking pose, 1969.

Tony Benn, December 1969.

The Labour government formed in March 1974. The front row includes Shirley Williams (far left), Michael Foot (second left), Harold Wilson (centre), James Callaghan (seventh left), followed by Roy Jenkins, Tony Crosland, Eric Varley and Barbara Castle.

James Callaghan, Labour Prime Minister 1976–9, seen here in 1979.

Michael Foot, Eric Heffer and Denis Healey, December 1980. At that time Foot and Healey were Leader and Deputy Leader of the Labour Party respectively.

Michael Foot, Labour Leader, receiving a kissing telegram from two scantily clad ladies, Stevenage, 1 June 1983.

Denis Healey, Labour Deputy Leader, attacking the Conservative government at a Labour Party press conference at Transport House, 6 June 1983, in the run-up to the 1983 general election.

Neil Kinnock, 41-year-old contender for the leadership of the Labour Party, in 1983.

John Smith, Labour Party Leader 1992–4. (John Chapman/National Museum of Labour History)

A young Tony Blair, Labour Party Leader 1994– and Prime Minister 1997–.

Secondly, it has sought to apply market-led forces to its economic and social strategies, with an emphasis being placed upon the state acting as an enabler rather than simply as a provider. Thirdly, its sympathies are essentially pro-European and pro-American. Fourthly, it is committed to brokering a peace in Northern Ireland. Fifthly, it has stressed the essential need for constitutional reform in such areas as the electoral system, the devolution of government, and changes in the House of Lords.

Ostensibly, New Labour is about communication and more open government. Blair has emerged as the great communicator and as a populist leader. This was most evident on 31 August 1997 after the death of Diana, Princess of Wales. His style tapped into the popular mood of sorrow throughout the nation at that time. In other areas, however, there has been less transparency than initially suggested. Indeed, David Clark was given the Cabinet post of Chancellor of the Duchy of Lancaster, with responsibility for brokering a Freedom of Information Act. In December 1997 a White Paper on the proposed Act was published; it indicated government thinking on the matter and dealt with national and local government, quangos (non-elected bodies dealing with the distribution of government money), the NHS, and privatized utilities. The anticipated Freedom of Information Act was to signal a new relationship between the government and the people by which access to information would be improved and an era of accountability would begin. None the less, since David Clark's removal from office, in the ministerial reshuffle of July 1998, the development of such an Act has slowed. Jack Straw, the Home Secretary, has taken responsibility for the Act, the first Bill of which, in May 1999, revealed that the government had withdrawn from its original position. While schools, local authorities and hospitals are to be more accountable it is clear that there will be exceptions where ministerial discretion will prevent unwarranted disclosure on the grounds that substantial harm might be done to the state. The commissioner to administer the Act will not be independent and government will not be forced to reveal how it arrives at policy decisions.[11] In effect, the intended all-embracing act will not be implemented.

The market-led nature of New Labour's approach, the second feature of Labour policy, was of course blatantly obvious in Brown's 1997 Budget, particularly in the explicitly titled programme of 'Welfare to Work'. It was also evident in the statement, in November 1998, that pledged that there would be a fundamental reform of the welfare state and proposed a tax credit scheme for poor working families. In December, as part of that strategy, the government pressed forward with a reduction in the benefits for lone parents, which led forty-seven Labour MPs to vote against the action, on a three-line whip, and for fourteen to abstain. The government in fact won by 457 votes to 107, with the support of the Conservatives.

Nevertheless, in January 1998 the government did announce a New Deal for unemployed 18 to 24-year-olds, to work with subsidized private employers, to have education or training, to set up in self-employment or a variety of other alternatives in its strategy to eliminate unemployment by the twenty-first century. In March 1998, Brown also announced a redistributive Budget strategy which included the introduction of a Working Family Tax Credit, from October 1999, a Disabled Persons Tax Credit, increases in child benefit, subsidies for employers to take on the long-term unemployed and extra spending in many other areas. Therefore, it has not been entirely clear that New Labour has played down the redistribution of income element, although its great adherence to market forces suggests that social differences may be widened rather than narrowed.

The philosophy behind New Labour seems to have been to reduce social need through an alliance between the state and the private sector. This was outlined, in some detail, by Tony Blair on 18 March 1999. The context of this was a government pledge to a twenty-year programme to eradicate child poverty. Blair suggested that a modern welfare state should be 'active, not passive, genuinely providing people with a hand-up, not a hand-out'.[12] Committing £6,000 million to help tackle child poverty in the course of the current Parliament, 'the quiet revolution', Blair suggested that there are six characteristics of a modern welfare state, They are, he said:

- tackling social exclusion, from decayed communities to drugs and unemployment;
- mutual responsibility, a hand-up, not a hand-out;
- help focused upon those who need it most;
- an end to fraud and abuse;
- public/private partnership on welfare, schools and health, not just benefits;
- a re-emphasis on active welfare, schools and health, not just benefits. . . .

He added that

> The third way in welfare is clear: not to dismantle it or to protect it
> unchanged but to reform it radically, taking its core values and
> applying them afresh to the modern world. . . . Poverty should not be
> a birthright. Being poor should not be a life sentence. We need to
> break the cycle of disadvantage so that children born into poverty
> are not condemned to social exclusion and deprivation. . . .
>
> There will always be a mixture of universal and targeted help. But
> one is not superior or more principled than the other.[13]

In effect, Blair's statement stressed that the state under New Labour
would become an enabler as well as a provider, helping people into jobs
as well as ensuring that their interests were protected. It was now in
partnership with, not hostile to, private industry.

Thirdly, as Peter Mandelson and Roger Liddle have stressed, New
Labour is committed to Europe. In government it has followed through
that commitment, recognizing that the European Economic
Community is responsible for half of British exports and for
guaranteeing about 3 million jobs in Britain. Despite the criticism of
William Hague, the Conservative Leader, and some hesitation about
joining a single European currency, New Labour is committed to
Europe. In October 1997, Gordon Brown announced that the
government favoured eventual entry into the European Monetary
Union but not in the lifetime of Blair's first Parliament and only if
agreed in a referendum.[14]

The British political and military alliance with the United States is
obvious. It is particularly evident in Blair's constant support for Bill
Clinton, the United States' President, in containing Saddam Hussein and
Iraq from military expansion, and in the close relationship that
developed between Britain and the United States in dealing with the
Yugoslavian government and the Kosovan refugee crisis throughout 1999.
Indeed, in the Kosovan crisis Blair took the lead in the NATO action
against the Serbian-dominated Yugoslavian state. In the case of Kosovo, in
particular, Blair seems to have carved out for himself the reputation of
being a major political player on the world stage.

On Ireland, the fourth area of activity, the Blair government offered
Sinn Fein, the Irish Republican political party, a meeting with officials to
discuss the preconditions for a renewed ceasefire in May 1997. By July

1997 the Irish Republican Army (IRA) had declared a ceasefire and Sinn Fein representatives were allowed to enter the Northern Ireland Assembly at Stormont, although not allowed to be involved in the peace-process discussions. In October 1997, Blair met Gerry Adams, the Sinn Fein Leader, and full-scale negotiations began. After many political twists, Blair focused the minds of all and gained an agreement on the Irish peace process, including provision for a Northern Ireland Assembly, a North–South Ministerial Council of the Isles at Easter 1998, and certain ceasefire conditions laid down as the basis for the peace talks known as the Good Friday Agreement. There still remains, however, the issue of implementing the agreement and the problem of decommissioning arms which both the Irish Republican Army and the Protestant paramilitaries seem reluctant to deliver.

The fifth major commitment of New Labour has been to constitutional and electoral reform. Such a commitment was first announced in the Queen's Speech in May 1997. In June it was revealed that the Liberal Democrats were being invited to take seats on the Cabinet committee to discuss constitutional reform, and other mutual interests. In December 1998 the Electoral Reform Commission was set up under Lord Jenkins, the former Labour minister and co-founder of the SDP. Lord Jenkins was set the task of devising a system of proportional representation for the Westminster elections in preparation for a referendum on the issue. In October 1998, Blair accepted its recommendation of an Alternative Vote Top-Up System of proportional representation for parliamentary elections and in June 1999 the election for European MPs was based upon a system of proportional representation, with electors voting for parties not individuals.

The Labour government has also created both a Scottish and Welsh Assembly in 1999, which allows for a greater representation of national minority-interest groups in an attempt to undermine the demands for political independence in both Scotland and Wales. And, in addition, there have been moves to modernize the monarchy and discussions about replacing the House of Lords by an assembly largely based on life-time peers and a much-reduced number of hereditary peers, en route to extinction.

The Blair government has certainly been hyperactive. Indeed, it is fair to argue that Blair has achieved the objective he set himself, at the 1997 Labour Party Conference, of making his administration 'one of the great reforming governments in British history'. Certainly, there have been constitutional, economic and welfare reforms in abundance. Most certainly, the direction of British politics has been changed. Nevertheless, one might question the direction of some of these reforms. While it is, perhaps, fair to suggest that the electoral and constitutional reforms will provide for wider participation in the politics of Britain it is still evident that there has been some downgrading of the proposed Freedom of Information Act and some feeling that true decision-making is becoming increasingly concentrated in the hands of the spin-doctors, such as Peter Mandelson, and government advisers.[15] In addition, there are many within Labour ranks who, while welcoming many of the reforms, are critical of the direction that they are taking and the Old Labour and socialist principles that they appear to be abandoning.

The resignation of Peter Mandelson as Secretary of Trade and Industry, a post he had been raised to in July 1998, over the issue of his mortgage arrangement was a welcoming sight to some Party members and MPs. Nevertheless, rumblings about the style of government which, apparently, relies upon 'cronies' and sees the appointment of friends as advisers, still continues.[16]

The main siren voice has been Roy Hattersley, the former Deputy Leader of the Labour Party, who, as early as July 1997, was declaring his lack of commitment to New Labour because of its desertion of policies to deal with the poor and for blatantly ignoring the need to redistribute wealth in order to move towards equality. The market-forces approach of both state and private enterprise is hardly going to redistribute wealth or create a fairer society. Although Hattersley's concerns are probably, now, partly allayed by a Blair commitment to eradicate child poverty and a further pledge to set a minimum wage of £3.00 per hour for 18 to 21-year-olds and of £3.60 per hour for those over 21.

CONCLUSION

As Britain enters the twenty-first century it is led by a Labour government with a strong reforming zeal, with a Leader, in Tony Blair, who is becoming the great communicator and populist figure. It is offering a wider participation in politics, more regional and local decision-making, closer links with Europe, a modern political society and, above all, the Third Way in British politics – uniting the state and private industry in tackling the social and economic problems of the nation. The present Labour government is thus far removed from its predecessors, with less dependence upon the trade unions and less emphasis upon the state intervening in the economy on its own to ensure full employment. In

Conclusion

The Labour Party emerged to win working-class and trade-union support from the Liberal and Conservative parties, and it was helped in this process by the intransigence of Old Liberalism and the emergence of socialist activities. As a result of the Taff Vale Case and other legal actions against trade unions, just under half of British trade unionists were connected to Labour before the First World War. There were 353,000 affiliated trade-union members in 1900, about 1,127,000 in 1908 and 1,451,000 in 1909, in the year which saw the affiliation of the Miners' Federation of Great Britain with more than 400,000 members. By 1914, the Labour Party had 1,895,000 members, of whom 1,858,000 were members of affiliated trade unions. The Labour Party was thus, overwhelmingly, a party of the trade unions.

Although the National Executive Committee of the LRC was, from the beginning, often dominated by socialists (from within and outside the trade-union movement) it is clear that Labour was not, initially at least, a socialist party. It did not become so until the introduction of the 1918 Constitution, which included Clause 3d, the famous Clause Four, which committed it to the public ownership of industry and services. Prior to that date, however, the LRC/Labour Party had been led by socialists, such as James Keir Hardie, James Ramsay MacDonald and Philip Snowden. Some, particularly Hardie, were collectivists who believed in the state ownership of the means of production while others, such as Snowden, believed that socialism was about guaranteeing freedoms and rights for the individual in a capitalist society which did not permit such rights through imposing long hours and low wages on its workforce. After 1918, of course, the Party was identified with Clause Four and the commitment to public ownership.

The First World War was, of course, a catalyst in Labour's development. Firstly, it divided the Liberal Party between the Asquithites and the Lloyd Georgeites. Secondly, it forced Labour to develop its socialism in order to distinguish itself from the Liberal Party. Indeed, the wartime experience was vital in defining the type of socialism that Labour introduced, for what it opted for was effectively an extension of the wartime controls of industry to permanent state control.

Nevertheless, Clause Four must not be allowed to dominate the way in which we perceive the Labour Party for Labour was essentially a party of the trade unions and, thus, the party of the working class. It might have been led by professional organizers and administrators, such as Ramsay MacDonald and Philip Snowden, but it was dominated by the trade unions who automatically returned thirteen of the twenty-three members of the National Executive Committee, and voted on the election of the rest.

The Labour Party did well out of the support of the trade unions and the working class, developing rapidly during the interwar years when it formed two minority administrations, in 1924 and between 1929 and 1931. Its organization improved dramatically and it is not true to suggest that its political success derived from the failure of the other two major political parties, particularly the Liberals.

In 1931, however, it faced a serious political setback when the economic crisis of the Wall Street Crash of 1929 reverberated around the world and helped increase unemployment to more than 3 million in Britain. The economic cost of this, and the resulting measures to reduce the Labour government's deficit, particularly the suggested 10 per cent cut in unemployment benefits, resulted in the split of the Labour Cabinet and the defection of Ramsay MacDonald, and some other Labour leaders, to the National government. The evidence suggests that MacDonald was driven to form the National government and that the accusation that he schemed to betray the Labour government/Party is simply not borne out by the evidence.

The collapse of the Labour Party in the 1931 general election did, of course, set it back a generation. However, it is clear that Labour was not fundamentally damaged by the political debacle of 1931. Labour had only lost about 1,700,000 votes, or about 20 per cent of its vote, and was back to its 1929 general election vote in 1935. The thing that had changed is that there was now a National government, bringing together the Conservatives, National Liberals and National Labour, against Labour, preventing it assuming power again.

During the nine years it was out of power, Labour strengthened its municipal and local position, developed its socialist agenda, particularly in relationship to public ownership. It also acquired a new leadership. Had there been no Second World War, and a general election in 1940, Labour would have improved its political position substantially but it is doubtful that it would have won. However, the Second World War provided it with new opportunities. While Labour refused to join Neville Chamberlain's wartime administration in 1939 it became part of the Winston Churchill wartime Coalition government in 1940, for which it was largely responsible. Labour's leaders, such as Clement Attlee, Ernest Bevin, Hugh Dalton and Herbert Morrison all gained valuable experience in the wartime government which paved the way for Labour's postwar success.

Labour won the first postwar general election in July 1945 and Attlee became Prime Minister of Labour's first majority government. To many, this administration was the high point for Labour. It saw the implementation of plans for public ownership, the creation of the modern welfare state and the formation of the National Health Service, its coping stone. While it is clear that the Beveridge Report of 1942 provided the basis for some of the actions of the Labour government of 1945–50, though not the Labour government of 1950–1, Labour was directly responsible for many of the social policies that were introduced, most obviously in its commitment to Nye Bevan's NHS.

By 1950, however, the Labour government was ailing. It has been suggested that this might have been because Labour's socialist policies put it ahead of the electorate, rather than with it or behind it. But whatever the situation, Labour was weakened by division and lost the 1951 general election, remaining in opposition for thirteen years during which there was great concern about its political future.

Although Labour did form governments in the 1960s and 1970s, it was in opposition for thirty-five out of the forty-six years between 1951 and 1997. Harold Wilson and James Callaghan led Labour administrations in the 1960s and 1970s, but they were not particularly successful and faced serious trade-union opposition in their attempts to impose wage controls. There were also genuine fears in the 1950s, 1980s and 1990s that Labour would never be able to form another government as its traditional working-class base declined and as society changed. Anticipating industrial change if not trade-union opposition, Hugh Gaitskell, Labour's Leader in the late 1950s and early 1960s, attempted to change the image of the Party by abandoning Clause Four but found the trade unions opposing him. The trade unions, by now diversifying into white-collar areas rather than declining at this point, were also responsible for the industrial unrest of the late 1970s, and the 'Winter of Discontent' of 1979, that led to the defeat of James Callaghan's Labour government in

1979. By the 1980s, wedded to Clause Four, the trade unions, high taxation, unilateralism, and an ever-expanding welfare state it appeared that Labour was unelectable. The 1983 general election was its low point, its worst political performance since 1918, when it was still an emerging political party.

The general election of 1983 was, however, a turning point. From that moment onwards, and through the successive leaderships of Neil Kinnock, John Smith and Tony Blair, the Labour Party moved to the right. Labour Leaders acted to reduce the influence of the trade unions and effectively abandoned Clause Four years before Tony Blair pushed for its formal rejection in 1994 and 1995. Labour began to abandon the image of being a working-class party. It also left behind the idea that the state could ensure that there was full employment, something foreshadowed by James Callaghan and Denis Healey at the time of the financial crisis in the mid-1970s. The unthinkable had happened, the welfare state was no longer sacrosanct.

Since then Tony Blair has forced Labour to go the whole hog and reduce the power of trade unions, abandon public ownership, reject unilateral disarmament, and create a new 'Third Way' in politics bringing both the state and private industry into a partnership for the future. In the year 2000, then, the Labour Party is fundamentally different from what it had been in 1918, 1945 or even 1983.

The Attlee governments had been about planning, social redistribution of wealth and income, and public ownership. The Blair government has enabled people to help themselves rather than simply provided public benefits out of high taxation. Blair's government is committed to winning support from across the political spectrum. Even to the Gaitskellite revisionists of the 1950s the redistribution of income and wealth were essential in a society designed to ensure that there was social justice and full employment, although Clause Four was not seen as vital. In contrast, Blair has rejected the redistribution of income, nationalization and full employment in the search for policies of economic growth that will appeal to all sections of British society.

One central issue in postwar Labour history has been Labour's relationship to the EEC. In 1961 it opposed entry, despite much division of opinion, largely because Gaitskell felt that he needed to protect Commonwealth interests. In 1966 and 1967 Wilson moved towards supporting a new application because of Britain's economic weakness, but this was vetoed by the French in May 1967. When the issue of membership was again revived in the early 1970s, with Edward Heath signing the Treaty of Accession in 1972 and Britain joining in 1973, it is clear that Labour was divided once again – with Roy Jenkins leading a rebellion of sixty-nine Labour MPs voting in favour of the EEC in October 1971. To maintain unity within the Party, Wilson decided that there would be a referendum in 1975, which favoured the renegotiated terms of the Treaty of Accession by a two to one majority. Since then, Labour had broadly supported the operation of the EEC while retaining within its midst sceptics, most notably Tony Benn. The problem of the EEC remains, however, since Tony Blair will have to make the decision of when Britain will enter the European Monetary Union, which will link all the currencies of the EEC together and lead to the Euro replacing the pound in Britain. In October 1997, Gordon Brown, the Chancellor of the Exchequer, announced that the Labour government favoured eventual entry but not in the lifetime of this Parliament and only if agreed in a referendum. Yet the poor showing of Labour in the European elections of June 1999 has made Labour think again about the need to campaign for Britain's entry into the European Monetary Union, although the commitment to a referendum on the matter is still being pressed forward. A *Guardian*/ICM poll, published on 14 July 1999, suggests that while 25 per cent would vote for joining the European single currency, 62 per cent would vote against and 13 per cent are 'Don't knows'. The promised referendum might be a long way off.

The Labour Party no longer resembles the organization it was in the past. It is no longer a socialist party, in the old sense of the word, but a political party of the centre. New Labour might win elections, and attract support from all the social classes but that is because it is now a progressive political party in the centre of British politics and no longer a party of the trade unions and the working class. Whether this can be sustained beyond the political life of its populist leader waits to be seen. Whatever happens, Tony Blair is faced with dealing with the major issues, most obviously those of joining the European Monetary Union and bringing peace to Northern Ireland by creating a working and effective Northern Ireland Assembly. Perhaps, as Tony Blair announced to the Labour Party Conference in September 1997, his administration will be 'one of the great reforming governments in British history'. Only time will tell.

Appendix 1

Leaders of the Labour Party

The post of Labour Leader is difficult to define before 1906, and in the Labour Representation Committee, J.R. MacDonald, as Secretary, and James Keir Hardie, as Leader of the Parliamentary Labour Group from 1904 onwards, both have the right to claim some type of leadership. From 1906 to 1921 the leading figures in the Labour Party were known as Chairman and Vice-Chairman of the Parliamentary Party; from 1922 to 1962 as Chairman and Leader of the Parliamentary Party and Deputy Leader; from 1970 to 1978 as Leader of the Parliamentary Party and Deputy Leader; and from 1978 onwards, as Leader and Deputy Leader of the Party.

LEADER

1906–8	James Keir Hardie
1908–10	Arthur Henderson
1910–11	George Barnes
1911–14	James Ramsay MacDonald
1914–17	Arthur Henderson
1917–21	William Adamson
1921–2	Joseph R. Clynes
1922–31	James Ramsay MacDonald
1933–2	Arthur Henderson
1932–5	George Lansbury
1935–55	Clement Attlee
1955–63	Hugh Gaitskell
1963–76	Harold Wilson
1976–80	James Callaghan
1980–3	Michael Foot
1983–92	Neil Kinnock
1992–4	John Smith
1994–	Tony Blair

DEPUTY LEADER

1906–8	David Shackleton
1908–9	George Barnes
1910–11	Joseph R. Clynes
1911–12	William Brace
1912–14	James Parker
1914–15	Arthur Gill
1915–18	John Hodge and George Wardle (joint)
1918–21	Joseph R. Clynes
1921–2	James Thomas and Stephen Walsh (joint)
1922–3	Stephen Walsh and Josiah Wedgwood (joint)
1923–31	Joseph R. Clynes
1931–5	Clement Attlee
1935–45	Arthur Greenwood
1945–56	Herbert Morrison
1956–9	James Griffiths
1959–60	Aneurin Bevan
1960–70	George Brown
1970–2	Roy Jenkins
1972–6	Edward Short
1976–80	Michael Foot
1980–3	Denis Healey
1983–92	Roy Hattersley
1992–4	Margaret Beckett
1994–	John Prescott

Appendix 2

Labour Party General Secretary
(Post known as Secretary until 1959)

1906–12	James Ramsay MacDonald
1912–35	Arthur Henderson
1935–44	J. Middleton
1944–62	Morgan Phillips
1962–8	A. Williams
1968–72	H. Nicholas
1972–82	Ron Hayward
1982–5	Jim Mortimer
1985–94	L. Whitty
1994–8	T. Sawyer
1998–	M. McDonagh

Appendix 3

Labour Votes and Parliamentary Seats in General Elections

Year		Votes	% of vote	Number of seats
1900		62,698	1.3	2
1906		329,748	5.9	30
1910 (Jan.)		505,657	7.6	40
1910 (Dec.)		371,802	6.4	42
1918	Coalition	161,521	1.5	10
	non-Coalition	2,245,777	20.8	57
1922		4,237,349	29.7	142
1923		4,439,780	30.7	191*
1924		5,489,087	33.3	151
1929		8,370,417	37.1	287*
1931	National Lab.	341,370	1.5	13
	Labour	6,649,630	30.9	52
1935	National Lab.	339,811	1.5	8
	Labour	8,325,491	38.0	154
1945		11,967,746	48.0	393*
1950		13,266,176	46.1	315*
1951		13,948,883	48.8	295
1955		12,405,254	46.4	277
1959		12,216,172	43.8	258
1964		12,205,808	44.1	317*
1966		13,096,629	48.0	364*
1970		12,208,758	43.1	288
1974 (Feb.)		11,645,616	37.2	301*
1974 (Oct.)		11,457,079	39.2	319*
1979		11,532,218	36.9	269
1983		8,456,934	27.6	209
1987		10,029,807	30.8	229

Year	Votes	% of vote	Number of seats
1992	11,559,857	34.4	271
1997	13,517,911	43.2	418*

* Labour government

Appendix 4

Shares of the Vote in General Elections in Great Britain 1918–97

Year	Conservatives	Labour	Lib/Alliance/Lib Dem.	Others
1918	55.9	23.7	14.4	6.0
1922	38.3	30.0	29.1	2.7
1923	37.8	31.1	30.1	1.0
1924	45.9	34.1	18.2	1.8
1929	37.5	37.9	23.6	1.0
1931	60.8	31.2	6.6	1.4
1935	53.2	38.6	6.8	1.4
1945	39.3	48.8	9.2	2.6
1950	43.0	46.8	9.3	0.9
1951	47.8	48.8	2.6	0.3
1955	49.3	47.3	2.8	0.6
1959	48.8	44.6	6.0	0.6
1964	42.9	44.8	11.4	0.9
1966	41.4	48.9	8.6	1.1
1970	46.2	43.9	7.6	2.3
1974 (Feb.)	38.8	38.0	19.8	3.4
1974 (Oct.)	36.7	40.2	18.8	4.3
1979	44.9	37.8	14.1	3.2
1983	43.5	28.3	26.0	2.2
1987	43.3	31.5	23.1	2.1
1992	42.8	35.2	18.3	3.8
1997	30.7	43.2	16.8	8.3

Appendix 5

Party Membership (000s)

Year	Individual members	Trade-union membership	Co-operative & socialist societies	Total
1900		353	23	376
1910		1,394	32	1,431
1920		4,318	42	4,360
1930	277	2,011	58	2,347
1935	419	1,913	45	2,378
1940	304	2,227	40	2,571
1945	487	2,510	41	3,039
1950	908	4,972	40	5,920
1955	843	5,606	35	6,484
1960	790	5,513	25	6,328
1965	817	5,602	21	6,440
1970	680	5,519	24	6,183
1975	675	5,750	44	6,392
1980	348	6,407	56	6,811
1985	313	5,827	60	6,227
1990	311	4,922	54	5,287

(Individual membership began in 1918 and no count was taken until 1928)

Appendix 6

Women MPs 1945–97

Year	Con.	Lab.	Other	Total	%
1945	1	21	2	24	3.8
1950	6	14	1	21	3.4
1951	6	11	0	17	2.7
1955	10	14	0	24	3.8
1959	12	13	0	25	4.0
1964	11	18	0	29	4.6
1966	7	19	0	26	4.1
1970	15	10	1	26	4.1
1974 (Feb.)	9	13	1	23	3.6
1974 (Oct.)	7	18	2	27	4.3
1979	8	11	0	19	3.0
1983	13	10	0	23	3.5
1987	17	21	3	41	6.3
1992	20	37	3	60	9.2
1997	15	101	6 (inc.)	122	18.2

Drawn from Lucy Peake, 'Women in the campaign and in the Commons', in Andrew Geddes and Jonathan Tonge (eds), *Labour's Landslide* (Manchester, Manchester University Press, 1997), p. 171.

Notes

INTRODUCTION

1. *Bradford Labour Echo*, 17 April 1897.
2. R. Moore, *The Emergence of the Labour Party 1880–1924* (London, Hodder and Stoughton, 1978), p. 61.

1. THE FOUNDATION OF THE LABOUR REPRESENTATION COMMITTEE, 1900, AND THE RISE OF LABOUR, *C.* 1900–18

1. For a detailed study of all these socialist and trade-union strands read Keith Laybourn, *The Rise of Socialism in Britain* (Stroud, Sutton, 1997).
2. *Report of the Conference on Labour Representation, Memorial Hall, 27 February 1900*, Chairman's report.
3. *Ibid.*, p. 10.
4. P. Clarke, *Lancashire and the New Liberalism* (Cambridge, Cambridge University Press, 1993), p. 139.
5. *The Times*, 27 September 1915.
6. John Burn's diary, 26 September 1915 (BM, Add. MSS, 46,337), quoted in Morgan, *Keir Hardie*, p. 277.
7. *Workman's Times*, 8 October 1892, 'The Coming Conference'.
8. *Bradford Labour Echo*, 20 April 1895.
9. Keir Hardie, open letter to John Burns, quoted in Emrys Hughes, *Keir Hardie's Speeches and Writings (from 1888 to 1915)* (Glasgow, Forward, 1928), pp. 99, 115.
10. *Labour Party Annual Conference Report, 1907*, Parliamentary Report, p. 37.
11. *Labour Leader*, 16 January 1906.
12. Johnson (ILP) Collection, British Library of Political and Economic Science, letter from J.R. MacDonald to J.B. Glasier, 21 July 1906.
13. J. Bruce Glasier diary (in the University of Liverpool Archives), 21 July 1906.
14. J. Bruce Glasier, *J. Keir Hardie MP: A Memorial* (Glasgow n.d.), p. 50.
15. *Labour Party Annual Conference Report, 1907*, p. 61.
16. *Ibid.*, p. 63.
17. Iain Maclean, *Keir Hardie* (London, Allen Lane, Penguin, 1975) p. 125.
18. J.R. MacDonald, *Ramsay MacDonald's Political Writings*, edited with an introduction by Bernard Barker (London, Allen Lane, Penguin, 1972).

19. J.R. MacDonald, *Socialism* (London, Social Problems Series, T.C. & E.C. Jack, 1907), p. 122.

20. C. Wrigley, 'Labour and the Trade Unions', in K.D. Brown (ed.), *The First Labour Party 1906–1914* (London, Croom Helm, 1985). Not all parts of Britain followed this trend as suggested by Sam Davies, *Liverpool Labour: Social and Political Influences on the Development of the Labour Party in Liverpool, 1900–1939* (Keele, Keele University Press, 1996).

21. Wrigley, 'Labour and the Trade Unions', in Brown (ed.), *The First Labour Party*, p. 142.

22. *Ibid.*, p. 152.

23. *Ibid.*, p. 151.

24. M.G. Sheppard and John L. Halstead, 'Labour's Municipal Election Performance in Provincial England and Wales, 1901–13', *Bulletin of the Society for the Study of Labour History*, 39 (1979), 42; Keith Laybourn and Jack Reynolds, *Liberalism and the Rise of Labour 1890–1918* (London, Croom Helm, 1984), pp. 109, 149.

25. J. Liddington and J. Norris, *One Hand Tied Behind Us* (London, Virago, 1984); A. Phillips, *Divided Loyalties* (London, Virago, 1987); S. Holton, *Feminism and Democracy* (Cambridge, Cambridge University Press, 1988).

26. C. Colette, *For Labour and For Women* (Manchester, Manchester University Press, 1989), p. 35.

27. Pamela M. Graves, *Labour Women: Women in British Working-class Politics 1918–1939* (Cambridge, Cambridge University Press, 1994).

28. Report of the Annual Conference of the Women's Labour League, in *League Leaflet*, March 1913, quoted in Graves, *Labour Women*, p. 9.

29. Colette, *For Labour and For Women*, p. 37.

30. Bill Lancaster, 'The Rise of Labour', *Labour History Review*, 57 (1992), 98, and Bill Lancaster, *Radicalism, Co-operation and Socialism: Leicester Working-class Politics 1860–1906* (Leicester, Leicester University Press, 1987).

31. Jack Reynolds and Keith Laybourn, *Labour Heartland: A History of the Labour Party in West Yorkshire During the Inter-war Years 1918–1939* (Bradford, Bradford University Press, 1987), p. 59.

32. Keith Laybourn, *The Rise of Labour: The British Labour Party 1890–1979* (London, Edward Arnold, 1988), chapter 2.

33. Location cited in text, p. 317.

34. E.P. Thompson, 'Homage to Tom Maguire', in Asa Briggs and John Saville (eds), *Essays in Labour History* (1960), pp. 276–316.

35. *Bradford Observer*, 28 April 1891.

36. *Yorkshire Factory Times*, 1 May 1891.

37. K.D. Brown, *The English Labour Movement* (London, Gill and Macmillan, 1982), p. 189.

38. James Hinton, *Labour and Socialism: A History of the British Labour Movement 1867–1974* (Brighton, Harvester, 1983), p. 81.

2. LABOUR AT WAR, 1914–18

1. *Bradford Pioneer*, 9 January 1914.
2. A. Marwick, *The Deluge* (London, Macmillan, 1975 edition); P. Abrams. 'The Failure of Social Reform, 1918–1920', *Past and Present*, 24 (1963); R. Miliband, *Parliamentary Socialism* (London, Merlin, 1972 edition); R. McKibbin, *The Evolution of the Labour Party 1910–1924* (Oxford, Oxford University Press, 1974); J.M. Winter, *Socialism and the Challenge of War 1912–1918* (London, Routledge & Kegan Paul, 1974).
3. 13 of the 23 NEC members were directly elected by trade unionists.
4. R. Harrison, 'The War Emergency Committee', in A. Briggs and J. Saville (eds), *Essays in Labour History* (London, Macmillan, 1971), pp. 211–59.
5. Winter, *Socialism and the Challenge of War*, p. 184.
6. *Ibid.*, pp. 187–8.
7. J.M. Winter, *Socialism and the Challenge of War* (London, Routledge & Kegan Paul, 1974), pp. 214–15.
8. Harrison, 'War Emergency Committee', p. 259.
9. Laybourn and Reynolds, *Liberalism and the Rise of Labour*, chapter 7.

3. RAMSAY MACDONALD AND THE RISE AND FALL OF THE LABOUR PARTY, 1918–31

1. Keith Laybourn, 'The Rise of the Labour Party and the Decline of Liberalism: The State of the Debate', *History*, 80, No. 259 (June 1995), 207–26.
2. Christopher Howard, 'Expectations Born to Death: Local Labour Party Expansion in the 1920s', in J. Winter (ed.), *The Working Class in Modern British History: Essays in Honour of Henry Pelling* (Cambridge, Cambridge University Press, 1983).
3. David Marquand, *Ramsay MacDonald* (London, Jonathan Cape, 1977).
4. Henry Pelling, *The Origins of the Labour Party* (London, Macmillan, 1954); R. McKibbin, *Evolution of the Labour Party* (Oxford, 1974); Clarke, *Lancashire and the New Liberalism*; M. Bentley, *The Climax of Liberal Politics: British Liberalism in Theory and Practice 1868–1918* (London, Edward Arnold, 1987); Tanner, *Political Change and the Labour Party* (Cambridge, Cambridge University Press, 1990).
5. Bill Lancaster, *Radicalism, Cooperation and Socialism: Leicester working-class politics 1860–1906* (Leicester, Leicester University Press, 1987).
6. Howard, Expectations, p. 81.
7. *Ibid.*, p. 65.
8. *Ibid.*, p. 78.
9. *Ibid.*, p. 74.
10. McKibbin, *Evolution*; B. Barker, 'Anatomy of Reform: The Social and Political Leadership of the Labour Leadership of Yorkshire', *International Review of Social History*, 18 (1973), 1–27.

11. McKibbin, *Evolution*, pp, 112–62, 243.
12. *The Times*, 6 December 1918.
13. Archives of the Labour Party, National Executive Committee, Minutes, June 1923.
14. Huddersfield Divisional Labour Party, Minutes, 23 July 1918.
15. Colne Valley Divisional Party, Minutes, 20 January, 1 May, 9 June 1917; *Leeds Weekly Citizen*, 19 April 1918.
16. Batley and Morley Divisional Labour Party, Minutes, 1931–3.
17. Labour Party, National Executive Committee, June 1918, February 1920, May 1920, March 1922.
18. *Bradford Pioneer*, 7 March 1919.
19. Graves, *Labour Women*, p. 1.
20. Labour Party, NEC, Minutes, 23 June 1919.
21. *Ibid.*, p. 85
22. Marion Phillips, 'Birth Control – A Plea for Careful Consideration', *Labour Women*, March 1924, p. 34; Graves, *Labour Women*, p. 86.
23. *Labour Party Conference Report, 1925* (London, Labour Party, 1925), p. 44.
24. Graves, *Labour Women*, p. 99.
25. Drawn from the minutes of the central Labour parties of Bradford, Halifax and Leeds for the 1920s. Also see Reynolds and Laybourn, *Labour Heartland*, p. 42.
26. *Labour Party Conference Report, 1935* (London, Labour Party, 1935), p. 179.
27. A. Booth, *British Economic Policy 1931–1949: Was there a Keynesian Revolution* (London, Harvester Wheatsheaf, 1989); S. Glynn and A. Booth, *The Road to Full Employment* (London, Allen & Unwin, 1987).
28. Lewis Minkin, *The Contentious Alliance: Trade Unions and the Labour Party* (Edinburgh, Edinburgh University Press, 1991), p. 1.
29. TUC, *Congress Report, 1925* (London, TUC, 1925), pp. 363–4.
30. W.M. Citrine, *The Trade Unions in the General Election* (London, TUC, 1931), p. 5.
31. TGWU *Record* (June 1931), p. 327 quoted in R. Shackleton, 'Trade Unions and the Slump', in Ben Pimlott and Chris Cook (eds), *Trade Unions in British Politics* (London, Longman, 1982), p. 123.
32. Reynolds and Laybourn, *Labour Heartland*, pp. 58–61, 158–61.
33. David Marquand, '1924–1932', in David Butler, *Coalitions in British Politics* (London, Macmillan, 1978), p. 52; Marquand, *MacDonald*, pp. 311–12.
34. *Labour Party Annual Conference Report, 1926* (London, Labour Party, 1926), p. 192.
35. PRO, 30/69, item 173, MacDonald diaries, 1910–37.
36. L. MacNeill Weir, *The Tragedy of Ramsay MacDonald* (London, Secker & Warburg, 1938), p. 383.
37. Marquand, *MacDonald*, p. 795.

38. *Ibid.*, p. 631.
39. Laybourn, *The Rise of Labour*, pp. 76–83.
40. TUC, General Council, Minutes, 20–1 August 1931.

4. THE COLLAPSE AND REVIVAL OF LABOUR, *C.* 1931–45

1. J. Stevenson and C. Cook, *The Slump* (London, Jonathan Cape, 1977), p. 107.
2. *Labour Party Conference Report, 1920* (London, Labour Party, 1920), pp. 181–3.
3. *Labour Party Conference Report, 1922* (London, Labour Party, 1922), pp. 222–3.
4. *Labour and the Nation* (London, Labour Party, 1928), p. 6.
5. *Labour Party Conference Report, 1928* (London, Labour Party, 1928), pp. 200–3, 212–15.
6. R.H. Tawney, *The Choice Before the Labour Party* (London, Socialist League, 1933); Sir S. Cripps, *Problems of a Socialist Government* (London, Gollancz, 1933).
7. L. Minkin, *Contentious Alliance: Trade Unions and the Labour Party* (Edinburgh, Edinburgh University Press, 1991), pp. 30–4.
8. Ben Pimlott, *Labour and the Left in the 1930s* (Cambridge, Cambridge University Press, 1977).
9. Ben Pimlott, *Hugh Dalton* (London, Macmillan, 1985), p. 206.
10. *Ibid.*, p. 213
11. David Howell, *British Social Democracy* (London, Croom Helm, 1976), p. 72.
12. *Ibid.*, p. 217–18.
13. NEC of the Labour Party, Minutes, 2 September 1924 outlines the whole issue from 1922 to 1924.
14. *Ibid.*, 23 September 1924.
15. *Ibid.*
16. N. Fishman, *The British Communist Party and the Trade Unions 1933–1945* (Aldershot, Scolar Press, 1995), p. 34.
17. *Class Against Class* (London, CPGB, 1929).
18. K. Laybourn and D. Murphy, *Under the Red Flag: A History of Communism in Britain 1849–1991* (Stroud, Sutton, 1999) provides a detailed study of relations between the CPGB and the Labour Party based upon the latest research.
19. *Ibid.*
20. T. Buchanan, *The Spanish Civil War and the British Labour Movement* (Cambridge, Cambridge University Press, 1991), p. 3.
21. *Daily Worker*, 4 February 1937.
22. Buchanan, *Spanish Civil War and the British Labour Movement*, chapters 5 and 6.
23. Reynolds and Laybourn, *Labour Heartland*; W. Gallacher, *Revolt on the Clyde* (London, Lawrence and Wishart, 1979 edition), chapter 11.
24. D. Blaazer, *The Popular Front & Progressive Tradition* (Cambridge, Cambridge University Press, 1992), pp. 148–54; Pimlott, *Labour and the Left in the 1930s*.

25. K. Morgan, *Against Fascism and War: Rupture and Constitution in British Communist Politics, 1935–1941* (Manchester, Manchester University Press, 1989), pp. 36, 131–3.

26. *Leeds Citizen*, 3 February 1939; Huddersfield Labour Party, Minutes, 21 February 1939; Halifax Labour Party, Minutes, 25 May 1939.

27. City of Leeds Labour Party, File 72/6, circular of Militant Labour League, Leeds branch, 24 September 1938, 28 December 1938, 8 May 1939.

28. Labour Party archives, LP/FAS/34/20.1.

29. P.M. Williams, *Hugh Gaitskell* (Oxford, Oxford University Press, 1982), p. 69.

30. B. Pimlott, *Labour and the Left in the 1930s*, pp. 77–99.

31. K. Harris, *Attlee* (London, Weidenfeld & Nicolson, 1982), p. 128.

32. R.M. Titmuss, *Problems of Social Policy* (London, HMSO, Longman Green, 1951), p. 508.

33. P. Addison, *The Road to 1945: British Politics and the Second World War* (London, Jonathan Cape, 1975), p. 118.

34. *Ibid.*, p. 271.

35. A. Calder, *The People's War* (London, Jonathan Cape, 1965); H. Pelling, *Britain and the Second World War* (London, Fontana, 1970); A. Marwick, *Britain in the Century of Total War* (London, Bodley Head, 1965); R. Miliband, *Parliamentary Socialism* (London, 1972); H.L. Smith (ed.), *War and Social Change: British Society and the Second World War* (Manchester, Manchester University Press, 1986).

36. C. Barnett, *The Audit of War: The Illusion and Reality of Britain as a Great Nation* (London, Macmillan, 1986); M. Beloff, *Wars and Welfare* (London, Edward Arnold, 1982).

37. K.O. Morgan, *The People's Peace* (Oxford, Oxford University Press, 1991), p. 17 suggests that there was no wartime consensus. This view is generally supported by B. Pimlott, 'The Myth of Consensus', in L. Smith (ed.), *Echoes of Greatness* (Basingstoke, Macmillan, 1988); and S. Brooke, 'The Labour Party and the Second World War', in A. Gorst, L. Johnson and W. Scott Lucas (eds), *Contemporary British History 1931–1961* (London, Pinter in association with the Institute of Contemporary British History, 1991).

38. Addison, *The Road to 1945*, p. 126.

39. Miliband, *Parliamentary Socialism*, p. 274.

40. G.D.H. Cole, *A History of the Labour Party since 1914* (London, Allen & Unwin, 1948), p. 380.

41. Labour Party, Policy Committee Minutes, 23 May 1941.

42. *Social Insurance and Allied Services*, report by Sir William Beveridge (London, HMSO, 1942); J. Harris, 'Some Aspects of Social Policy in Britain during the Second World War', in W.J. Mommsen (ed.), *The Emergence of the Welfare State in Britain and Germany* (London, Croom Helm, 1981).

43. K. Harris, *Attlee* (London, Weidenfeld & Nicolson, 1982).

44. *Ibid.*, p. 220.

45. *Ibid.*, p. 223.
46. *Ibid.*, pp. 227–30.
47. *Ibid.*, p. 231.
48. H. Dalton, *The Second World War Diary of Hugh Dalton 1940–45*, ed. B. Pimlott (London, Jonathan Cape, 1986), pp. 455, 538, 564.
49. *Labour Party Conference Report, 1935* (London, Labour Party, 1935), p. 158.
50. Addison, *The Road to 1945*, p. 261.

5. THE HIGH POINT OF LABOUR; THE ATTLEE GOVERNMENTS, 1945–51

1. P.M. Williams, *Hugh Gaitskell* (Oxford, Oxford University Press, 1979); Harris, *Attlee*; J. Campbell, *Nye Bevan and the Mirage of British Socialism* (London, Weidenfeld & Nicolson, 1987).
2. H. Pelling, *The Labour Governments 1945–1951* (London, Macmillan, 1984); K.O. Morgan, *Labour in Power 1945–1951* (Oxford, Clarendon Press, 1984); Peter Hennessy, *Never Again: Britain 1945–51* (London, Jonathan Cape, 1992).
3. Addison, *The Road to 1945*; Miliband, *Parliamentary Socialism*.
4. H. Gaitskell, *The Diary of Hugh Gaitskell*, ed. P.M. Williams (London, Jonathan Cape, 1983), pp. 173–4.
5. *Ibid.*, p. 15.
6. *Ibid.*, p. 14.
7. The Labour Party, *Labour Believes in Britain* (London, Labour Party, 1949).
8. K. Laybourn, *The Labour Party 1881–1951: A Reader in History* (Gloucester, Sutton, 1988), chapter on 'The Attlee Years, 1945–1951', pp. 123–48, which refers to records of Cabinet meetings and the records of the Lord President of the Council office.
9. *The Times*, 26 September 1949.
10. A. Bevan, *In Place of Fear* (London, Heinemann, 1952), p. 80.
11. Morgan, *Labour in Power 1945–1951*, p. 79.
12. A. Bullock, *The Life and Times of Ernest Bevin, Vol. 1: Trade Union Leader 1881–1940* (London, Heinemann, 1960); A. Bullock, *The Life and Times of Ernest Bevin, Vol. II, Minister of Labour 1940–1945* (London, Heinemann, 1967); A. Bullock, *Ernest Bevin: Foreign Secretary* (London, Heinemann, 1983), pp. 478–9, 549–85.
13. Bullock, *Ernest Bevin: Foreign Secretary*, p. 672.
14. Pelling, *Labour Governments 1945–1951*, p. 128.
15. Keep Left Group Minutes, 28 July 1949 to 27 February 1951, to be found in the Jo Richardson Papers at the Labour Party Archives, Manchester, and scattered throughout the Ian Mikardo Papers, also in the Labour Party Archives, 103 Princess Street, Manchester.
16. *Tribune*, 20 May 1949.

17. J. Schneer, *Labour's Conscience: The Labour Left 1945–51* (London, Unwin Hyman, 1988) p. 58.
18. R.H.S. Crossman, M. Foot and I. Mikardo, *Keep Left* (New Statesman, London, 1947), pp. 38, 40–1. There is a copy in the Ian Mikardo Papers (partly merged with the Jo Richardson Papers), at the Labour Party Archives.
19. *Ibid.*, p. 40.
20. *Ibid.*, pp. 76–7.
21. Ian Mikardo Papers and Correspondence, Group Paper 75, 'Report on talk with Pandit Nehru, 20 September 1950', written by Fenner Brockway, 22 January 1951.
22. *Daily Herald*, 8 August 1947.
23. *Ibid.*, 13, 22, 29 August and 5, 12 September 1947; cuttings, Michael Foot Papers, P 3.
24. *Tribune*, 20 May 1949.
25. Jo Richardson Papers, Labour Party Archives at Manchester, Keep Left Group Minutes. The first meeting, erroneously put down as being held in 1948, was actually convened on 27 July 1949 and at it other regular meetings were inaugurated.
26. *Ibid.*, Minute 21, 7 September 1949.
27. *Ibid.*, 31 August 1949.
28. *Ibid.*, 7 September 1949.
29. Jo Richardson Papers, Keep Left Group Minutes, 11 July 1950.
30. Schneer, *Labour's Conscience*, pp. 196–8.
31. Jo Richardson Papers, Keep Left Group Minutes, 8 March 1950.
32. *Ibid.*, 6 and 7 October 1950 refer to the ideas (item/res. 225) that several Brains Trusts should be held each year). The meeting of 31 October 1950 listed several such meetings. The Mikardo Correspondence is full of organizational material connected with these meetings.
33. R.H.S. Crossman, *The Backbench Diaries of Richard Crossman*, ed. J. Morgan (London, Hamish Hamilton and Jonathan Cape, 1981), p. 196; E. Shaw, *Discipline and Discord in the Labour Party* (Manchester, Manchester University Press, 1988), p. 37.
34. Jo Richardson, Keep Left Minutes, 29 September 1949 and 1 March 1950.
35. *Ibid.*, 14 March 1950.
36. *Ibid.*, 19 January 1951 and 30 October 1951.
37. *Ibid.*, 26 April 1951 records Bevan, Freeman and Wilson among the fifteen members present.
38. Mikardo Correspondence contains an undated listing of forty-seven names plus Lord Faringdon, Lord Silkin, Tom Balogh and Dudley Sears.
39. Mikardo Correspondence, Group Paper 14, 'Plan for Mutual Aid'. The Jo Richardson Papers also include a map of the distribution and majority of the seats of the Keep Left Group members.

40. Schneer, *Labour's Conscience*, chapter 7 on 'The Labour Left and the Constituencies' and p. 188.

41. Mikardo Correspondence, National Museum of Labour History, Manchester.

42. Mikardo Correspondence, Keep Left Group Minutes and Records.

43. *Ibid.*

44. Jo Richardson and Ian Mikardo Papers, for 1952, contain the five-page petition of the MPs.

45. The General Secretary's Papers (Morgan Phillips), Box 4, 'Lost Sheep Files', GS/LS/49 to GS/LS/72 contains the accusations levelled against Bevan and the minutes of meetings.

46. Schneer, *Labour's Conscience*, chapter 5.

47. I. Mikardo, *Ian Mikardo: Back Bencher* (London, Weidenfeld & Nicolson, 1988), pp. 118–19.

6. CRISIS IN THE LABOUR PARTY, 1951–79

1. Laybourn, *The Rise of Labour*.

2. Crossman, *The Backbench Diaries of Richard Crossman*, pp. 28, 31.

3. TUC Annual Conference, *Report*, 1951, Appendix A, pp. 475–525; *Labour Party Annual Conference, Report*, 1953, pp. 61–80.

4. Crossman, *Backbench Diaries*, p. 396.

5. Gaitskell, *Diary*, pp. 383, 385–94.

6. Crossman, *Backbench Diaries*, pp. 402–5, 411–12. Also, the National Museum of Labour History contains the Labour Party file on these events which indicates the intense nature of the debate on Bevan's position.

7. Crossman, *Backbench Diaries*, p. 614.

8. *Ibid.*, p. 615.

9. K. Jefferys, *Anthony Crosland: A New Biography* (London, Richard Cohen Books, 1999).

10. S. Haseler, *The Gaitskellites: Revisionism and the British Labour Party, 1951–1964* (London, Macmillan, 1969), chapter 5, pp. 99–111.

11. C.A.R. Crosland, 'The Transition from Capitalism', in R. Crossman (ed.), *New Fabian Essays* (London, Turnstile Press, 1952), p. 38.

12. P.M. Williams, *Hugh Gaitskell* (Oxford, Oxford University Press, 1982), p. 324.

13. M. Phillips, *Labour in the Sixties* (London, Labour Party, 1960), p. 15.

14. M. Abrams, R. Rose and R. Hinden, *Must Labour Lose?* (London, Penguin, 1960).

15. Haseler, *The Gaitskellites*, p. 228; B. Brivati, 'Hugh Gaitskell and the EEC', *Socialist History*, 4, Spring 1994, 16–32.

16. *Labour Party Annual Conference Report*, 1962, p. 30.

17. Labour Party, *Signposts for the Sixties* (London, Labour Party, 1966), p. 7.

18. However, some were achieved, most notably Tony Crosland's 10/65 Minute

which paved the way for the introduction of comprehensive schools and the phasing out of direct grant grammar schools.

19. *In Place of Strife: A Policy for Industrial Relations*, Cmnd 3888, paragraphs 93–6.
20. *Labour Party Conference Report, 1971*, p. 165.
21. B. Castle, *The Castle Diaries 1974–1976* (London, Weidenfeld & Nicolson, 1980), pp. 85, 121, 124, 224, 252–6.
22. Tony Benn, *Against the Tide: Diaries 1973–6* (London, Hutchinson, 1989), p. 188, entry 28 June 1974.
23. *Ibid.*, p. 189.
24. James Callaghan, *Time and Chance* (London, Fontana, 1987), p, 426.
25. A.J. Taylor, *The Trade Unions and the Labour Party* (London, Croom Helm, 1987), pp. 101–3.
26. *Guardian*, 20 February 1976.

7. DESPAIR, RECONSTRUCTION AND REVIVAL: THE LABOUR PARTY FROM FOOT TO BLAIR, 1979–94

1. Anthony Heath, Roger Jewell, John Curtice and Bridget Taylor (eds), *Labour's Last Chance? The 1992 Election and Beyond* (Aldershot, Dartmouth, 1994); Abrams, Rose and Hinden, *Must Labour Lose?*
2. Denis Healey, *The Time of My Life* (Harmondsworth, Penguin, 1990), pp. 465–84.
3. *Ibid.*, p. 484.
4. T. Grant, *The Unbroken Thread – The Development of Trotskyism over 40 Years* (London, 1989); A. Smith, *Faces of Labour – The Inside Story* (London, 1996); J. Callaghan, *British Trotskyism* (Oxford, Blackwell, 1984); J. Callaghan, *The Far Left in British Politics* (Oxford, Blackwell, 1987); M. Crick, *The March of Militant* (London, Faber, 1986); P. Taafe and T. Mulhearn, *Liverpool: A City that Dared to Fight* (London, 1988).
5. K. Laybourn, *British Trade Unionism* c. *1770–1990; A Reader in History* (Stroud, Sutton, 1991), p. 213.
6. *Guardian*, 25 July 1983.
7. *Ibid.*, 15 March 1984.
8. *Labour Party Conference Report, 1985* (London, Labour Party, 1985), p. 128.
9. *Observer*, 6 October 1986.
10. *Guardian*, 14 August 1986.
11. *Ibid.*, 3 December 1986.
12. *Ibid.*, 6 March 1987.
13. Pippa Norris, 'Labour Party Factionalism and Extremism', in Heath, Jowell, Curtice and Taylor (eds), *Labour's Last Chance?*, particularly pp. 73–8.
14. *Ibid.*, pp. 77–6.

15. *Guardian*, 2 October 1989.
16. *It's Time to Get Britain Working Again* (London, Labour Party, 1992), p. 11.
17. *Ibid.*, p. 26.
18. Anthony Heath and Roger Jowell, 'Labour's Policy Review', in Heath, Jowell, Curtice and Taylor (eds), *Labour's Last Chance?*, p. 206.
19. *Today*, 11 April 1992.
20. *Sun*, 11 April 1992.
21. *Daily Telegraph*, 11 April 1992.
22. Ivor Crewe and Anthony King, 'Did Major Win? Did Kinnock Lose? Leadership effect in the 1992 election', in Heath, Jowell, Curtice and Taylor (eds), *Labour's Last Chance?*, p. 144.
23. *Guardian*, 25–7 March 1992.
24. *Ibid.*, 2 April 1992.
25. In June 1994 I visited Teresa Gorman MP in connection with a second-year History work placement student who was working in her office. Despite indicating to her my Labour credentials she expressed the view that the Conservative Party would lose the general election if Blair was returned, and favoured the election of John Prescott.

8. New Labour and Labour in Government, 1994–2000

1. Peter Mandelson and Roger Liddle, *The Blair Revolution: Can New Labour Deliver?* (London, Faber & Faber, 1996), chapter 1.
2. G. Radice and S. Pollard, *More Southern Discomfort* (London, Fabian Society, 1993), p. 16.
3. *Observer*, 30 April 1999.
4. *Guardian*, 18 and 23 May 1995.
5. Mandelson and Liddle, *The Blair Revolution*, p. 1.
6. *Ibid.*, pp. 3–4.
7. *Ibid.*, p. 17.
8. Philip Cowley, 'The Conservative Party, Decline and Fall', in Andrew Geddes and Jonathan Tonge (eds), *Labour's Landslide* (Manchester, Manchester University Press, 1997), p. 51.
9. *New Statesman*, 24 January 1997, also quoted in Steven Fielding, 'Labour's Path to Power', in Geddes and Tonge (eds), *Labour's Landslide*, p. 26.
10. Steven Fielding, 'Labour's path to power', in Andrew Geddes and Jonathan Tonge (eds), *Labour's Landslide*, pp. 23–35.
11. *Guardian*, 25 May 1999, article by Hugo Young.
12. *Ibid.*, 19 March 1999.
13. *Ibid.*
14. This statement was reiterated by Tony Blair at Prime Minister's Question Time, in the House of Commons, on 9 June 1999.

15. Andy McSmith, 'Knives Out for New Labour's Sycophants and Spinners: Blairite Guru Turns on Toadies', *Observer*, 23 May 1999.

16. Martin Bright and Anthony Barnett, 'Blunkett accused over jobs for cronies. Plum post of lobbyist friends fuels controversy over New Labour appointment', *Observer*, 23 May 1999, deals with the appointment of a man who worked with David Blunkett as a researcher, and worked as a lobbyist with Westminster Strategy for two years before being made a special adviser, and sixty-six such appointments by the Labour government.

Short Bibliography

There are thousands of books and articles which have dealt with the Labour Party during the twentieth century. Below are listed a few that will be of use to the general, rather than narrowly specialist, reader. These are published in London unless otherwise indicated.

J. Adams, *Tony Benn* (1992)

P. Adelman, *The Rise of the Labour Party 1890–1979* (3rd edition, 1996)

S. Brooke, *Labour's War: The Labour Party During the Second World War* (Oxford, 1992)

A. Bullock, *The Life and Times of Ernest Bevin*, 3 vols (1960, 1967, 1983)

J. Campbell, *Nye Bevan and the Mirage of British Socialism* (1987)

——, *Roy Jenkins: A Biography* (1983)

B. Castle, *The Castle Diaries 1974–1976* (1980)

C. Collette, *For Labour and for Women: The Women's Labour League 1906–1918* (Manchester, 1989)

C. Cook and I. Taylor (eds), *The Labour Party: An Introduction to its History, Structure and Politics* (1980)

R. Coopey, S. Fielding and N. Tiratsoo (eds), *The Wilson Governments 1964–1970* (1993)

M. Cowling, *The Advent of Labour 1920–24: The Beginning of Modern British Politics* (Cambridge, 1971)

I. Crewe and A. King, *SDP: The Birth, Life and Death of the Social Democratic Party* (Oxford, 1995)

M. Crick, *The March of Militant* (1986)

C.A.R. Crosland, *The Future of Socialism* (1956)

B. Donoghue, *Prime Minister: The Conduct of Politics under Harold Wilson and James Callaghan* (1987)

B. Donoghue and G. Jones, *Herbert Morrison: Portrait of a Politician* (1973)

M. Foot, *Aneurin Bevan 1897–1945* (1962)

——, *Aneurin Bevan, 1945–1960* (1973)

A. Geddes and J. Tonge (eds), *Labour's Landslide: The British General Election 1997* (Manchester, 1997)

P.M. Graves, *Labour Women: Women in British Working-class Politics 1918–1939* (Cambridge, 1994)

H. Harmer, *The Longman Companion to the Labour Party, 1900–1998* (1999)

K. Harris, *Attlee* (1985)

A. Heath, R. Jewell, J. Curtice and B. Taylor (eds), *Labour's Last Chance? The 1992 Election and Beyond* (Aldershot, 1994)

R. Heffernan and M. Marquese, *Defeat from the Jaws of Victory: Inside Kinnock's Labour Party* (1992)

P. Hennessy, *Never Again: Britain 1945–51* (1992)

——, and Anthony Seldon (eds), *Ruling Performance: British Governments from Attlee to Thatcher* (1987)

K. Jefferys, *The Labour Party since 1945* (1993)

——, *The Attlee Governments 1945–1951* (1992)

K. Laybourn, *The Rise of Labour: The British Labour Party 1890–1979* (1988)

——, *Philip Snowden* (1988)

——, *The Rise of Socialism in Britain c. 1881–1951* (Stroud, 1997)

——, and Dylan Murphy, *Under the Red Flag: A History of British Communism 1849–1991* (Stroud, 1999)

F. M. Leventhal, *Arthur Henderson* (Manchester, 1989)

P. Mandelson and R. Liddle, *The Blair Revolution: Can New Labour Deliver?* (1996)

D. Marquand, *Ramsay MacDonald* (1977; new edition, 1997)

R. McKibbin, *The Evolution of the Labour Party 1910–1924* (Oxford, 1974)

A. McSmith, *John Smith* (1994)

I. Mikardo, *Back-Bencher* (1989)

R. Miliband, *Parliamentary Socialism* (2nd edition, 1972)

L. Minkin, *The Labour Party Conference: A Study in the Politics of Inter-Party Democracy* (1978)

——, *The Contentious Alliance: Trade Unions and the Labour Party* (Edinburgh, 1991)

J. Morgan (ed.), *The Backbench Diaries of Richard Crossman* (1981)

K.O. Morgan, *Keir Hardie: Radical and Socialist* (1975)

——, *Labour in Power* (1983)

——, *Labour People, Leaders and Lieutenants* (Oxford, 1987)

——, *The People's Peace* (Oxford, 1990)

——, *Callaghan: A Life* (1997)

R. Pearce, *Attlee* (1997)

H. Pelling, *A Short History of the Labour Party* (11th edition, 1996)

B. Pimlott, *Labour and the Left in the 1930s* (Cambridge, 1977)

——, *Hugh Dalton* (1985)

——, *Harold Wilson* (1992)

E. Shaw, *The Labour Party since 1979: Crisis and Transformation* (1994)

——, *The Labour Party since 1945* (Oxford, 1997)

D. Tanner, *Political Change and the Labour Party* (Cambridge, 1990)

A.J. Taylor, *Trade Unions and the Labour Party* (1987)

A. Thorpe, *The British General Election of 1931* (Oxford, 1991)

——, *A History of the British Labour Party* (1997)

N. Tiratsoo (ed.), *The Attlee Years* (1991)

P. Williams, *Hugh Gaitskell* (1979)

J.M. Winter, *Socialism and the Challenge of War: Ideas and Politics in Britain 1912–18* (1974)

C.J. Wrigley, *Arthur Henderson* (Cardiff, 1990)

Index